EMILY BRONTË

NICK HOLLAND

First published 2018

The History Press
The Mill, Brimscombe Port
Stroud, Gloucestershire, GL5 2QG
www.thehistorypress.co.uk

British Library Cataloguing in Publication Data.
A catalogue record for this book is available from the British Library.

ISBN 978 0 7509 7898 9

Typesetting and origination by The History Press
Printed and bound in Great Britain by TJ International Ltd

CONTENTS

ACKNOWLEDGEMENTS

I entered university in the autumn of 1989, and found that the first book on my reading list was Emily Brontë's *Wuthering Heights*. I was mesmerised from the opening page, and that weekend I made my first visit to the Brontë Parsonage Museum in Haworth, where I purchased a framed picture of Emily, and Elizabeth Gaskell's biography of Charlotte. My lifelong obsession with the Brontës had commenced, but little could I know where it would lead. I want to sincerely thank all the people who have made it possible for me to write my own biography of Emily Brontë, over a quarter of a century later.

Thanks go to my incredibly supportive family and friends, especially to Jenny Hall for a gift that proved immensely welcome and helpful. Thanks also to all at The History Press for their hard work and encouragement.

Thank you to the many individuals and places who have been of great assistance, including all the staff and volunteers at the Brontë Parsonage Museum, Stephen and Julie at Ponden Hall, the Fleece Inn at Haworth, Leeds University and the Brotherton Library, the British Library in London, John Hennessy, Cornwall Council, the Brussels Archives, the Hollybank Trust (once Roe Head School) and Sandra at the Brontë School House in Cowan Bridge (formerly the Clergy

Daughters' School, it is now a self-catering guest house and a much more agreeable place to stay than in Carus Wilson's time).

I also want to thank all the people who have supported my website www.annebronte.org, a true labour of love, and those who have followed me so supportively on Facebook and Twitter, where you will find me named @Nick_Holland_. Finally, thanks go to you, the reader. I hope you enjoy my work and that it encourages you to return to the truly great work of the Brontës.

PREFACE

Emily Brontë will forever be remembered as the author of *Wuthering Heights*. Published in 1847, the year before Emily's death, aged just 30, it is her only novel, and yet it remains a must-read for people across the world, and has been translated into nearly thirty languages.

For many people, *Wuthering Heights* is the greatest novel ever written, and yet it should not be forgotten that Emily Brontë was also a poet of the first order. It was the discovery of Emily's hidden book of poetry, by her sister Charlotte in September 1845, that led to the Brontë sisters' first venture into print. *Poems by Currer, Ellis and Acton Bell* was the result, and it would lead on to the novels by Emily, Charlotte and Anne that are so loved today.

Emily contributed twenty-one poems to the collection, and we now know of over 200 poems by her. This figure is complicated somewhat, as some of these 'poems' are mere fragments consisting of a few lines, while other individual poems may have been intended to join with others to take longer forms. It is also beyond doubt that much of Emily's poetic output has now been either lost or destroyed, possibly by Charlotte after Emily's death, or by Emily Brontë herself.

Nevertheless, we can see that Emily was a very prolific poet, and much of what she wrote is very good indeed. Emily is commonly thought of today as the greatest Brontë poet, even though Anne was the only sister to have her poetry published independently during her lifetime. Charlotte, certainly, was astonished at how good Emily's poetry was, as she revealed in her *Biographical Notice of Ellis and Acton Bell* when describing the discovery of her sister's work: 'I looked it over, and something more than surprise seized me – a deep conviction that these were not common effusions, nor at all like the poetry women generally write.'

This statement is very revealing – Charlotte had read much of Emily's poetry, but had seen nothing like this work before. The truth is that Emily wrote two kinds of poetry, and accordingly had two books in which she collected her poems. The first book contained Gondal poetry, that is poetry pertaining to the people and land of Gondal, the island kingdom that she created as a child with her younger sister Anne, and which Emily in particular would continue to write about throughout her life.

Emily also wrote about her deeper feelings, however, and these are the wild and vigorous poems that Charlotte talks about. These poems dealt with faith, with death, with love, with despair – with the very fabric of life itself. Always a very private person, even with her own family, Emily kept this particular collection of poems well hidden, or so she thought. The discovery of her secret poems sent her into a fury, and she would only consent to publish them if her identity could be hidden from the reading public.

Emily's poetry can present a similar problem to us today. It is difficult to ascertain whether some of her verses are purely connected to Gondal, or whether she is examining her own feelings and life within them. In many of her verses, the two sides of her creativity are inextricably intertwined.

As Emily grew older, she retreated more and more into her imaginary world of Gondalian intrigue and adventure, until the lines between fiction and reality became blurred. Even her overtly Gondal-based poetry, then, can actually tell us a lot about Emily herself.

Emily Brontë remains an enigmatic figure: the shy Yorkshire-born daughter of an Irish priest, seemingly unable or unwilling to fit in with the wider world around her, and yet her writing is wild and exciting, powerful and full of life. Getting to the heart of Emily is no easy task; we have only two letters of hers still extant, and her prose writing is not largely biographical, as her sister Anne's novels often were.

It is in Emily's poems, however, that we can often discover an insight into her thoughts and feelings, those emotions that she always strived to keep hidden away. In this volume, we will take a look at twenty of Emily Brontë's greatest poems, and examine how they illuminate episodes from her life, and that of the family around her. Taking a broadly chronological approach, in that we will start with her birth in Thornton and end after her tragic yet courageous death in Haworth three decades later, we will use her poems to illustrate important themes and events in her life. From her days as a teacher, through her journey to Brussels, her passion for the moors, and the death of her brother Branwell, Emily's verse provides the perfect accompaniment and illumination.

It may never be possible to say with certainty how Emily felt, or how she lived from day to day, but by looking at these wonderful verses we can gain fascinating glimpses of the woman behind some of the nineteenth century's most enduring writing. Her work contains incredible stories, but the life of the author herself is just as incredible, in its own way. Emily Brontë was never a 'coward soul', but a visionary woman who refused to conform to anything other than her own ideas of what was right and what was wrong.

1

SMILING CHILD

Tell me, tell me, smiling child,
What the past is like to thee?
An Autumn evening soft and mild,
With a wind that sighs mournfully.
Tell me, what is the present hour?
A green and flowery spray,
Where a young bird sits gathering its power,
To mount and fly away.
And what is the future, happy one?
A sea beneath a cloudless sun,
A mighty, glorious, dazzling sea,
Stretching into infinity.

('Past, Present, Future', dated 14 November 1839)

E MILY BRONTË WAS 21 years old when she wrote her short poem 'Past, Present, Future'. She was not yet the genius who would write *Wuthering Heights*, but her verse already showed many of the themes that would dominate her writing: a yearning for the past, the supremacy of nature, and visions of the future, visions of death and the eternity to follow.

Emily writes of the past as a smiling infant, but this is not any child – it is a remembrance of herself. When we think of Emily Brontë today we think of an insular yet powerful woman, one whose might with a pen belied her timidity in real life. It is easy to think of Emily as downcast, morose even, but while these terms may indeed be applicable to some of Emily's life, they do not apply to the whole of her thirty-year existence. In her infancy, Emily was a smiling, happy child, a pretty girl doted upon by a loving family. It was an idyllic beginning full of promise, and one looked back upon fondly by Emily in the opening lines of her poem.

Thornton is a village around 4 miles from the city of Bradford, in what is now the county of West Yorkshire. It is surrounded to the south by moorland, and one property with a perfect view of the moors was Kipping House. The large and elegant house was home to the Firth family, heads of Thornton society and with the money to enjoy a life that most of the village's inhabitants could only dream of.

The head of the household was John Firth, the village doctor. His first wife died in 1814 after a tragic accident that saw her thrown from a horse, but in 1815 he married his second wife, Anne. Also at the house was John's daughter, Elizabeth, and she kept a diary detailing dinner parties, social gatherings, shopping trips, charitable work and more. It is in this diary, in an entry dated 30 July 1818, that the 21-year-old Elizabeth writes, 'Mrs J. Horsfall called. Emily Jane Brontë was born.'[1] This is the first record of Emily Brontë in print, but of course it was far from the last. Elizabeth Firth was to become an influential figure in the lives of the Brontës: a friend to Emily's parents, a benefactor at times of need, godmother to Anne, and, as we shall see, a potential stepmother to the Brontë siblings.

Emily and her sisters, Charlotte and Anne, are to many the Queens of Yorkshire, and indeed they bring tourists from across the world, flocking to one particular western outpost of the county. They are also often thought of as being prim and proper examples of Victorian womanhood, but while this description may be applied to Charlotte Brontë, and to an extent Anne, although she was more willing to challenge the values of Victorian society within her writing, it could never be a description of the free-spirited and independent-minded Emily.

We need to go back a little further to get an idea of where Emily's belligerence and rebelliousness come from. To discover Emily's roots, and the beginnings of the Brontë family as a whole, we have to leave the churchyards of Yorkshire behind and look in upon an eighteenth-century elopement on the banks of the River Boyne. Emily's father, Patrick Brontë, was a priest in the Church of England; it was a highly respectable position, if not necessarily a lucrative one, but of course he was neither born in England nor with the surname Brontë. The story is well known of how Patrick changed his surname to Brontë from the Irish Brunty, or perhaps Prunty, upon his arrival at St John's College, Cambridge University, in 1802.[2] The change in name was eventually adopted by his family in Ireland as well, including Emily's grandfather, Hugh, who shared many characteristics in common with her.

Hugh Brunty's story is unclear, even confusing, at many points, with associated legends that are now impossible to prove or disprove – obscured by the mists of time, and the sparsity of written records in eighteenth-century Ireland. Perhaps the most enduring myth, or possibly truth, about Hugh was that he was raised not by a Brunty at all, but by a cuckoo in the nest who had been brought from Liverpool – much like Heathcliff in Emily's great novel. This account was brought to light by a late nineteenth-century treatise, *The Brontës in Ireland* by Dr William Wright. Wright based his book upon eyewitness accounts, and the stories of people who had known Patrick Brontë and his family, although it reads like an intoxicating mixture of fact and fiction, truths and half-remembered tales.

Patrick's great-grandfather was a farmer and cattle dealer near Drogheda in County Louth, in what is now the Republic of Ireland, and he often travelled to Liverpool to sell cattle at the burgeoning market there. One of Wright's sources recalled how the farmer came to adopt a helpless child:

> On one of his return journeys from Liverpool a strange child was found in a bundle in the hold of the vessel. It was very young, very black, very dirty, and almost without clothing of any kind. No one on board knew whence it had come, and no one seemed to care what became of it. There was no doctor in the ship, and no woman except Mrs. Brontë, who had accompanied her husband to Liverpool. The child was thrown on the deck. Some one said, 'Toss it overboard'; but no one would touch it, and its cries were distressing. From sheer pity Mrs. Brontë was obliged to succour the abandoned infant ... When the little foundling was carried up out of the hold of the vessel, it was supposed to be a Welsh child on account of its colour. It might doubtless have laid claim to a more Oriental descent, but when it became a member of the Brontë family they called it 'Welsh'.[3]

The author goes on to describe how Welsh Brunty, as he was known, elopes and marries his master's daughter, Mary, in secret, and after being evicted wreaks revenge upon the family. Later he approaches one of his brothers-in-law and persuades him to let him adopt his son Hugh. Hugh is treated appallingly by Welsh, but eventually escapes and flees to the north of Ireland. This is supposedly the tale of the early years of Emily's grandfather, Hugh Brunty, later Brontë, and the account has obvious similarities to *Wuthering Heights* – but is this because it was made up by either Wright or his source, or because it was a family folktale that Emily knew and drew upon?

We get a rather different account of Hugh from Patrick himself. Writing to Elizabeth Gaskell as she prepared to commence her biography of Charlotte Brontë, Patrick stated:

> He [Patrick's father, Hugh] was left an orphan at an early age. It was said that he was of ancient family ... He came to the north of Ireland and made an early but suitable marriage. His pecuniary means were small – but renting a few acres of land, he and my mother by dint of application and industry managed to bring up a family of ten children in a respectable manner.[4]

One undisputed fact about Hugh was that he fell in love with Alice McClory from County Down. They wanted to marry, but there was a seemingly insurmountable obstacle in their way – Hugh was a Protestant and Alice was a Catholic. They eloped, and after a clandestine marriage in Magherally Church they set up home in a two-roomed cottage near Emdale in the parish of Drumballyroney. The cottage in County Down can still be visited today and has become a place of pilgrimage for Brontë fans, as it was here, just a year after the wedding of Hugh and Alice, that their first son was born. Born on St Patrick's Day, 1777, he was named Patrick after the saint, and was to become patriarch of perhaps the most famous family in world literature.

Patrick, as he revealed in his letter to Mrs Gaskell, was the first of a large family and, recognising the financial burden upon his parents, he was determined to make his own way in life from an early age. They were, by necessity, a poor family, but hard working and one that was nourished with love. Patrick's younger sister Alice commented on this at the age of 95 in 1891: 'My father came originally from Drogheda.

He was not very tall but purty stout; he was sandy-haired and my mother fair-haired. He was very fond to his children and worked to the last for them.'[5]

We also hear that Hugh Brunty was renowned as a wonderful storyteller, and it is likely to have been at Hugh's knee that Patrick developed his own love of stories and of books. It was this love of literature that changed his life forever. Patrick was training as a weaver, but one day a passing minister, Reverend Andrew Harshaw, heard the young boy reading aloud from Milton's *Paradise Lost.*[6] So impressed was the priest that he offered to give Patrick free tuition at a school he ran.

Patrick proved himself such an able scholar that by the age of 16 he was master of his own school. His prodigious talents as a scholar and schoolmaster came to the attention of another Anglican priest, the Reverend Thomas Tighe of Drumballyroney.[7] Tighe was a wealthy man, and hired Patrick to be tutor to his children. Once again, Patrick's scholarly prowess, hard work and pious nature impressed those around him. Tighe recognised that this young Irishman from a humble background could have a career within the Church, if he received a little help along the way. Thanks to Tighe's connections and money, Patrick Brontë was offered and accepted a scholarship at Cambridge University and a vocation to the priesthood. It was a stellar rise for a man who would otherwise have seen out his years working on a farm or as a weaver.

After graduating from Cambridge, Patrick was ordained as a deacon in 1806, and then as a priest in 1807. He served as an assistant curate in a number of parishes in the south of England, until in January 1809 he became assistant curate at All Saints' Church in Wellington, Shropshire. He remained in the parish for less than a year, but it was in Shropshire that he made a very important friendship – that of local schoolmaster, John Fennell.

In December 1807, Patrick moved north to the parish of Dewsbury in Yorkshire. It was part of the 'heavy woollen area', a booming district that was being transformed by the Industrial Revolution and the mills and factories that it brought. By 1811, Patrick received his first curacy, at the village of Hartshead on the hills outside Dewsbury. This was a momentous occasion for Patrick, and within a year he also gained a position as an examiner in the classics at a local school.

John Fennell of Shropshire had moved to Yorkshire as well, and had founded a school at Rawdon, near Leeds. Discovering that his friend Patrick was nearby, and knowing his reputation as an excellent Latin and Greek scholar, he enlisted his help. Also at the school were John's wife, Jane Fennell, their daughter, also called Jane, and their niece, Maria Branwell. She soon became the focal point of Patrick's visits to the establishment.

Maria was from Penzance on the south-western tip of Cornwall, where she was born into a large and prosperous merchant family in 1783. However, by the time Patrick met Maria her fortunes had declined; her parents, Thomas and Anne, had both died and she was now looking to make her own way in the world by helping at her aunt's school. Maria was in her late twenties, and Patrick in his mid-thirties,[8] but they fell rapidly in love.

On 29 December 1812 they were married in Guiseley Parish Church near Leeds. At the same ceremony, Maria's cousin, Jane Fennell, married Reverend William Morgan, a Welshman and close friend of Patrick. It was a joyous day, a double celebration, and Patrick and Maria may have had a premonition of William Morgan baptising their children in the years to come. This is a role he indeed fulfilled, but all too soon Morgan also had to preside over the funerals of many of them.

At the beginning of 1814 their first child was born, a daughter named Maria after her mother. A year later she was joined by a sister, Elizabeth Brontë. With a growing family, Patrick and Maria began to look for a new parish that offered a greater salary and more convenient living quarters, which is why, in May 1815, they moved to Thornton. In effect, the parishes of Thornton and Hartshead were involved in an ecclesiastical swap. Thornton's curate wanted to be nearer to Huddersfield as he had fallen in love with Frances Walker, of Lascelles Hall near the town.

The arrangement was greatly to the benefit of Patrick and Maria, as Thornton came with its own grace and favour parsonage building on the town's Market Street, whereas at Hartshead they had to rent a cottage on a farm. Thornton Parsonage is no longer owned by the Church of England, and although it may not be as famous as a certain parsonage building in Haworth, it is still well worth a visit. It is now an elegant café and delicatessen with an Italian theme, but it also contains items of interest to Brontë lovers, including its centrepiece – the early nineteenth-century fireplace by which the three writing sisters were born. Patrick may not recognise the building if he saw it today, but he would certainly recognise the name, as it has been named after his fifth child, and one who graced the building as an infant – 'Emily's'.

Patrick and Maria Brontë, like many newly married couples of the time, had children on an almost annual basis, but unlike the majority of their contemporaries all their children survived childbirth and infancy. The first child born in Thornton was named Charlotte, after one of Maria's sisters, and a year later, in 1817, their first and only son was born and christened Patrick, after his father. Patrick would always be known by his middle name to his family, taking on the maiden name of his mother – Branwell. In the male-dominated world of the early nineteenth century it would have been expected that Branwell would one day become the family's breadwinner, and that he would also support his sisters prior to their marriages, but it was a burden of expectation that he would find impossible to bear.

In the summer of 1818 the fifth child of Patrick and Maria was born; a child who was destined to write possibly the greatest novel of all time, as well as being one of the most remarkable poets of her day. From Elizabeth Firth's diary, we know that the child's name had already been decided on the day of her birth, but even in the choice of name, Emily differs from her other siblings, just as she was to prove to be different in many other ways as she grew into a strong-willed and independent woman.

Emily Jane Brontë was the only Brontë daughter to be given a middle name, with Jane presumably being chosen as a tribute to both Maria's cousin and the aunt who had played a role in bringing her and her husband Patrick together. Both Janes, Fennell and Morgan, would act as godmothers to the girl. The choice of Emily has to remain a mystery, as there is no record of an Emily among either the Cornish or Irish relatives; this makes Emily the only Brontë not named after a parent, aunt or, in Anne's case, after her grandmother. It seems fair to surmise that a woman named Emily must have been a friend known to Patrick and Maria, and a special one at that, whose name was given precedence over the Jane that would have been a more traditional choice in the family.

Emily Brontë started her life with a mystery, and she was to become a lover of mysteries, a creator of mysteries, and an enigma herself. Emily was a smiling and much-loved child, but as her poem reveals, even at an early age there was a mournful wind blowing through her life – a sighing breeze that would ever remind her of the early loss of her mother and two eldest sisters.

2

THE SILENT DEAD

I see around me tombstones grey,
Stretching their shadows far away.
Beneath the turf my footsteps tread,
Lie low and lone the silent dead –
Beneath the turf – beneath the mould –
Forever dark, forever cold –
And my eyes cannot hold the tears,
That memory hoards from vanished years,
For Time and Death and Mortal pain,
Give wounds that will not heal again –
Let me remember half the woe,
I've seen and heard and felt below,
And Heaven itself – so pure and blest,
Could never give my spirit rest –
Sweet land of light! thy children fair,
Know nought akin to our despair –
Nor have they felt, nor can they tell,
What tenants haunt each mortal cell,
What gloomy guests we hold within –
Torments and madness, tears and sin!

Well – may they live in ecstasy,
Their long eternity of joy;
At least we would not bring them down,
With us to weep, with us to groan,
No – Earth would wish no other sphere,
To taste her cup of sufferings drear;
She turns from Heaven with a careless eye,
And only mourns that we must die!
Ah mother, what shall comfort thee,
In all this boundless misery?
To cheer our eager eyes a while,
We see thee smile; how fondly smile!
But who reads not through that tender glow,
Thy deep, unutterable woe:
Indeed no dazzling land above,
Can cheat thee of thy children's love.
We all, in life's departing shine,
Our last dear longings blend with thine;
And struggle still and strive to trace,
With clouded gaze, thy darling face.
We would not leave our native home,
For *any* world beyond the Tomb.
No – rather on thy kindly breast,
Let us be laid in lasting rest;
Or waken but to share with thee,
A mutual immortality –

('I See Around Me Tombstones Grey', dated 17 July 1841)

As a young infant, Emily Brontë grew up surrounded by love, doted over by her oldest sisters, Maria and Elizabeth, and finding ready companions not much older than herself in Charlotte and Branwell. A happy life full of potential seemed to stretch before her, but as Emily's poetry shows more than the writings of any of her sisters, a dark shadow was ever hanging over the fate of the Brontës.

It has to be said that many of Emily Brontë's poems deal with dark, despairing themes. Death often forms the backdrop, as in 'I See Around Me Tombstones Grey', and, in some cases, becomes a character in its own right: brooding, waiting, inescapable. It is testimony to the childhood events that shaped Emily's life more than any other, the early losses that would haunt her dreams and imagination until they found release in her verse and in her great novel.

By the start of 1820, Thornton Parsonage was becoming increasingly crowded for the Brontë family. As well as Emily, her three sisters and her brother, and Patrick and Maria Brontë, there were the family servants, Nancy and Sarah Garrs. Nancy Garrs arrived at the parsonage aged just 13 shortly after the birth of Charlotte, having been trained at the Bradford School of Industry for Girls: a charitable organisation which helped the children of poor parents. Her younger sister, Sarah, was also a graduate of this school, and she was recruited to join her sister at Thornton Parsonage shortly after Emily's birth, with Nancy being promoted from nursemaid to cook and assistant housekeeper.

A contemporary account of the Bradford School for Industry reveals the very different background that the Garrs had compared to the Brontës, and also details the education they received:

The scholars, who are chosen by the subscribers, are taken in at eight years of age; and are taught to sew, knit, and read. They have materials to work upon found free, and the profits of their labours are expended in clothing them. The scholars also attend the school on the Sunday, and are taught to read and the Church Catechism, and attend church. Many excellent maid-servants have been reared in this school.[1]

Nancy and Sarah Garrs played an important role in Emily's infancy and, although they later married and moved away, they retained links to the Brontë family and remembered the children fondly.

The year 1820 saw two pivotal events that changed the Brontë story forever. On 17 January, Emily's beloved sister Anne was born. Anne Brontë was the sixth and final child of Patrick and Maria, and while she was ever to prove a blessing to Emily, her arrival made Thornton Parsonage even more crowded. In a letter sent to his friend Richard Burn just ten days after Anne's birth, Patrick wrote, 'There is, it's true, besides this a very ill constructed Parsonage House, which is not only inconvenient, but requires, annually, no small sum to keep it in repair.'[2]

It would seem fortunate for all concerned, then, that Patrick and his family would soon be moving to a new parish with a much larger parsonage building: the parish of Haworth. Its long-standing curate, Reverend James Charnock, had died in early 1819, and the Vicar of Bradford, Reverend Henry Heap, wrote to Patrick to offer him the job, as Haworth was then a sub-parish of Bradford itself. Unfortunately, Heap had failed to consult Haworth's Council of Elders, who had the traditional right of nominating their own parish priest, and they let it be known that they would not accept the imposition of Reverend Brontë upon them. Mindful of this impasse, Patrick politely declined the job offer,[3] tempting though it was.

Heap's next move was to give the post to Reverend Samuel Redhead, who had often stood in for Reverend Charnock during his final illness and seemed to be liked by the Haworth parishioners. This proved a great mistake. The story is told of how the parishioners turned violently against Reverend Redhead,[4] at one point sending a drunken man into the church on the back of a donkey, and on another occasion chasing him out of the village in fear of his life.

It had by now become clear to Henry Heap that the villagers would not accept any curate foisted upon them, and that a compromise would have to be reached. In an act of diplomacy, it was agreed that the parish elders would nominate the original choice, Patrick Brontë, who would then be confirmed in the post by the Vicar of Bradford. In this way, pride and tradition were upheld, and the Brontës found themselves moving to their new parish in April 1820.

Two carts carried the family and their possessions on the undulating journey across the moors separating Thornton and Haworth. Emily was approaching her second birthday at the time, and we can imagine the bleak, majestic landscape capturing her eye. It was her first extended view of the moorland scenery that would become so well known to her – a moment of epiphany in her life. Unfortunately, Haworth was to bring another such moment just a year later.

The move to Haworth seemed to be a propitious one at first. The parsonage building was much larger, and Patrick's salary increased too. Patrick was kept busy by the demands of this larger parish, it was true, but he was never a man to shun hard work. Maria also revelled in her new environment, raising her children with love and care at the same time as meeting the social demands that came with being the curate's wife. Everything was bright in the Brontë household, but it was about to be shaken to its core.

The first winter at the Haworth Parsonage saw Emily and her siblings all catch scarlet fever. It was to be the first of many illnesses that they would suffer in the unhealthy atmosphere of the moor-side village, a place where epidemics swept away a significant number of the populace year upon year. The children all recovered on this occasion, but another family member was about to be struck down with something far worse, as Patrick recalled in a letter to Reverend John Buckworth, the man who had brought him to Yorkshire eleven years earlier:

> I was in Haworth, a stranger in a strange land. It was under these circumstances, after every earthly prop was removed, that I was called on to bear the weight of the greatest load of sorrows that ever pressed upon me. One day, I remember it well; it was a gloomy day, a day of clouds and darkness, three of my little children were taken ill of scarlet fever; and, the day after, the remaining three were in the same condition. Just at that time death seemed to have laid his hand on my dear wife in a manner which threatened her speedy dissolution. She was cold and silent and seemed hardly to notice what was passing around her ... A few weeks afterwards her sister, Miss Branwell, arrived, and afforded great comfort to my mind.[5]

On 29 January 1821 a sudden change had come upon Mrs Brontë. Whereas the day before she had carried out her maternal duties as usual, on this day she collapsed to the floor, overtaken by unbearable pain in her stomach. Doctors were called for, but Maria's condition continued to worsen until it seemed obvious that things could end but one way. It was at this point that Maria's sister, Elizabeth Branwell, left her Cornwall home and moved into the Haworth Parsonage. At first, she nursed her sister – later, she would nurse and raise the children. Elizabeth, who became known as Aunt Branwell to her nephew and nieces, had sacrificed all that she had known when she entered the Haworth Parsonage in the summer of 1821. She would never see Cornwall again.

Elizabeth Branwell was not the only newcomer to the parsonage at this time, as Patrick paid for a nurse to be brought in for his wife. This was one of his many desperate outlays at this time – expenses that would have left him destitute if it had not been for the kindness of friends, who later paid off his debts. One such gift, of the substantial sum of £50, was sent to him by 'a benevolent individual, a wealthy lady, in the West Riding of Yorkshire'.[6]

The new nursemaid was not to Patrick's liking and was eventually dismissed, and she is perhaps most known today as the previously anonymous individual responsible for the unfounded tales of Patrick in Elizabeth Gaskell's biography of Charlotte Brontë: tales of how he never fed his children meat and his explosive temper. It was the nursemaid's revenge, and although she has long remained unnamed, recent research has revealed her to be Martha Wright (née Heaton). While her testimony regarding Patrick is less than reliable, she does provide a description of Emily at just 3 years old:

> Maria [that is the daughter Maria, then aged 7] would shut herself up in the children's study with a newspaper, and be able to tell one everything when she came out; debates in parliament, and I don't know what all. She was as good as a mother to her sisters and brother. But there never were such good children … they were good little creatures. Emily was the prettiest.[7]

Patrick had spared no effort or expense in seeking help for the wife he loved, but it was all in vain. Maria Brontë died after a terrible prolonged illness on 15 September 1821, aged 38. It is commonly thought today that she died of uterine cancer, but this may not be the actual cause of her death. The known details surrounding her demise were examined in 1972 by Professor Philip Rhodes, a Brontë lover and one of the foremost experts in this medical field, being then the professor of obstetrics and gynaecology at St Thomas' Medical School in London. Professor Rhodes concluded that Maria's death was brought on by haemorrhage and infection after the birth of Anne a year earlier, or a chronic inversion of the uterus. He writes:

The ultimate cause of death in both instances would be cardiac failure due to the anaemia. Of course there is an outside possibility of cancer of some organ within the abdomen, but it is unusual for this to occur before the age of forty. Certainly genital cancer would be very unlikely when the previous normality of reproductive function was so well displayed.[8]

Aged just 3, Emily's lack of years would have given her some defence against the grief caused by losing one's mother as a child, but she would still have felt the loss as she grew older, even if she would find it hard to remember her face, or the Cornish lilt in her voice. Emily's remembrance of this early loss can perhaps be seen in *Wuthering Heights*, with the first Cathy dying in childbirth and unable to see her daughter grow up.

Maria Brontë was the first of the Brontës to be buried under the cold flagstones of St Michael and All Angels Church – the same flagstones Emily would have to walk over every Sunday. While her mother did not have one of the grey tombstones referred to in her poem, she did not have to look far to see many such monuments as the window of her childhood bedroom, a room she shared with Charlotte as a girl, looked directly out onto the graveyard below. It was already a crowded graveyard by the time Emily and her family arrived in Haworth, and the epidemics that regularly struck the village saw it grow further still. Throughout her childhood, she would have become familiar not only with the sight of these monumental neighbours, the granite and stone edifices of death, but also with the sound of picks and shovels creating new graves.

Maria Brontë's last words are reported as being, 'Oh God – my poor children',[9] and it was perhaps this heartfelt exclamation which persuaded her sister Elizabeth that her place was now at the parsonage until the children were fully grown. One of the roles that Aunt Branwell took on was that of educator to the girls, teaching them scripture, as well as the needlework that would be expected to serve a dual purpose in their future lives. Money was often tight in the Brontë household, and Emily and her sisters would be expected to make their own clothing and mend existing clothing until it was finally beyond the point of repair; needlework was also an essential skill for a governess to teach her pupils, and both Patrick and Elizabeth must have assumed that this was the most likely career path for the sisters.

Patrick Brontë was a firm believer in the power of education – the transforming power that had taken him from Ireland to Haworth, via Cambridge University – but unlike many of his contemporaries, he believed that education could be of benefit to girls as well as boys. It was for this reason that Patrick wrote to his bank on 10 November 1824:

> Dear Sir, I take this opportunity to give you notice that in the course of a fortnight it is my intention to draw about twenty pounds out of your savings bank. I am going to send another of my little girls to school, which at the first will cost me some little – but in the end I shall not lose.[10]

The little girl that he was sending to school on this occasion was Emily Brontë, but unfortunately for Patrick, Emily and the family, he had made a major miscalculation – one that would see him lose most grievously. The school he was sending Emily to join, and where three of her sisters already waited, was called the Clergy Daughters' School at Cowan Bridge, but it has become infamous in literature as the deadly Lowood School attended by Jane Eyre.

Maria and Elizabeth Brontë had made the journey to Cowan Bridge on 1 July of the previous year, with Charlotte joining them there on 10 August. Maria and Elizabeth had previously enjoyed a term at Crofton Hall School near Wakefield, a prestigious establishment for girls that had once counted Elizabeth Firth among its pupils, but even though Elizabeth had made a contribution towards the school costs for Maria and

Elizabeth, it was beyond Patrick's means to keep them there or to send his three other daughters after them in their turn.

Cowan Bridge seemed an ideal compromise. Founded by the Reverend Carus Wilson in Westmorland, what we now know as Cumbria, it offered subsidies for the children of poor clergymen like Patrick. He would have expected that his children would be given a solid education in the skills they would need to be governesses and of course that they would be looked after while they were there, but Cowan Bridge was run on very different lines.

Carus Wilson was an arch-Calvinist; he believed in discipline and the importance of punishment, and considered that hardships on Earth were good for the soul. Charlotte Brontë, who would never forget the terrible scenes she witnessed at the school, would always insist that Lowood was an accurate portrayal of Cowan Bridge, that, if anything, it was even worse than she portrayed, with its lack of food, freezing conditions, arbitrary punishments and death ever lurking in its sick bays.

It is well known how Maria Brontë, the bright yet untidy girl with such promise, was treated especially harshly at the school, and how she is represented by the saintly Helen Burns in *Jane Eyre*, but, in contrast to this, Emily Brontë received very different treatment on her arrival at Cowan Bridge. Emily was the forty-fourth pupil at the school, and at just over 6 years old she was the youngest. In fact, the oldest pupils at the school were in their twenties, and only four were aged under 10 – three of those four being Elizabeth, Charlotte and Emily Brontë.

Nevertheless, Emily's academic talents impressed her schoolmasters, who recorded her accomplishments upon entry as 'reads very prettily and works a little'. The 'work' referred to is needlework, and this report on Emily is the most glowing given to any pupil in the Clergy Daughters' School records.[11] By contrast, Charlotte is described as 'writes indifferently

... Knows nothing of grammar, geography, history or accomplishments'. Maria's description is, 'Writes pretty well. Ciphers a little. Works badly.'

Emily, aged 6, obviously had winning ways, in contrast with the reserved woman she was to become, with her pretty looks and pleasing voice (later to be remarked upon by family friend John Greenwood) gaining approval from the often-harsh staff at the school. The school's superintendent, Miss Evans, later recalled how Emily's tender years and nature led to her being treated more favourably than others, calling her 'A darling child, under five years of age, [who] was quite the pet nursling of the school'.[12]

Even so, there were two dread events to come that even Emily's youth and pet status could not protect her from: she had to observe at first hand the demise and death of the two elder sisters she so looked up to. Charlotte Brontë described what happened in a mournful scene within *Jane Eyre*:

> That forest-dell, where Lowood lay, was the cradle of fog and fog-bred pestilence; which, quickening with the quickening spring, crept into the Orphan Asylum, breathed typhus through its crowded schoolroom and dormitory, and, ere May arrived, transformed the seminary into a hospital ... Many, already smitten, went home only to die: some died at school and were buried quietly and quickly; the nature of the malady forbidding delay.[13]

The Clergy Daughters' School was indeed a place where death and disease were rife, with malnourished pupils falling prey to cholera, typhoid and consumption. Five girls were sent home from the school in 'ill health', as their records refer to it, on 14 February 1825. One of them was Maria Brontë – she would die in Haworth of tuberculosis on 6 May. By the end of May, Elizabeth had also been sent home, where she rapidly declined and died on 15 June.

Maria was buried under the church floor next to her mother of the same name, with Elizabeth alongside them. Patrick had seen enough, and quickly fetched Charlotte and Emily back to Haworth to be taught by him and their aunt in the safety of their own home.

What effect did these early deaths have on Emily Brontë? The answer can be found in the way her life progressed, and in her poems and prose. Emily was a bright, loving and sensitive child who would ever carry around with her this deep grief from infancy. It was this childhood trauma that began to transform Emily from a talkative, charming girl into an intensely shy and private woman, and it was this memory that, as we shall see, led to Emily's near fatal pining on the next occasion she was sent to a school.

These are, as in Emily's poem at the head of this chapter, the everlasting tears that memory hoards from vanished years; these are the wounds that will not heal again. By just 6 years old, Emily Brontë had lost her mother and two eldest sisters, so it is little wonder that she would turn to death and graveyards time and time again throughout her life as a writer. There is also a touching tribute to her sister Maria in *Wuthering Heights*, if we choose to see it. Branwell was a talented and yet mischievous child. On stormy nights, and there are many of those on the edges of the Haworth Moors, he would tease his sisters that he could hear the departed Maria moaning in the wind. Emily would not forget this, as the ghostly encounter near the beginning of her novel shows:

'Let me in – let me in! … I'm come home: I'd lost my way on the moor!'

'I'll never let you in, not if you beg for twenty years!'

'It is twenty years,' mourned the voice: 'twenty years. I've been a waif for twenty years!'[14]

Emily Brontë wrote these words in 1845 – twenty years after the death of her sister Maria.

3

BURSTING THE FETTERS
AND BREAKING THE BARS

High waving heather 'neath stormy blasts bending,
Midnight and moonlight and bright shining stars,
Darkness and glory rejoicingly blending,
Earth rising to heaven and heaven descending,
Man's spirit away from its drear dungeon sending,
Bursting the fetters and breaking the bars.
All down the mountain sides wild forests lending,
One mighty voice to the life-giving wind,
Rivers their banks in their jubilee rending,
Fast through the valleys a reckless course wending,
Wider and deeper their waters extending,
Leaving a desolate desert behind.
Shining and lowering and swelling and dying,
Changing forever from midnight to noon;
Roaring like thunder, like soft music sighing,
Shadows on shadows advancing and flying,
Lightning-bright flashes the deep gloom defying,
Coming as swiftly and fading as soon.

('High Waving Heather 'Neath Stormy Blasts Bending', dated
13 December 1836)

THE DEATH OF their mother Maria had two pronounced effects on the Brontë children, which intensified with the procession of years. Firstly, they were drawn even closer as siblings, becoming all and everything to each other. While they revelled in each other's company, and sought each other out for solace and comfort, this also had the effect of making them less than welcoming of people from outside their own family unit.

Even with their own father, they could be reserved and secretive, so that although he would hear the sounds of their happy games from the seclusion of his study, when he entered the dining room he would find them suddenly quietened. Nevertheless, Patrick could tell from an early age that he had no ordinary children, and that they were developing characters and beliefs of their own. Realising that the shyness and reserve of his children was preventing him from finding out their true thoughts and feelings, he came up with an intriguing plan – by hiding them behind a mask he would encourage them to give answers that they would otherwise keep deep within themselves. He explained what happened next to Elizabeth Gaskell:

When my children were very young, when as far as I can remember, the oldest was about ten years of age, and the youngest about four, thinking that they knew more than I had yet discovered, in order to make them speak with less timidity, I deemed that if they were put under a sort of cover I might gain my end; and happening to have a mask in the house, I told them all to stand and speak boldly from under the cover of the mask.

I began with the youngest (Anne, afterwards Acton Bell) and asked what a child like her most wanted; she answered, 'Age and experience'. I asked the next (Emily, afterwards Ellis Bell) what I had best do with her brother Branwell, who was sometimes a naughty boy; she answered, 'Reason with him, and when he won't listen to reason, whip him'. I asked Branwell what was the best way of knowing the difference between the intellects of men and women; he answered, 'By considering the difference between them as to their bodies'. I then asked Charlotte what was the best book in the world; she answered, 'The Bible'. And what was the next best; she answered, 'The Book of Nature'. I then asked the next [Elizabeth] what was the best mode of education for a woman; she answered, 'That which would make her rule the house well'. Lastly, I asked the oldest [Maria] what was the best mode of spending time; she answered, 'By laying it out in preparation for a happy eternity'.[1]

Six short questions with short replies and yet very revealing about the characters of the Brontës as children, especially when it comes to the answer from Emily. Patrick chose his questions carefully, with each one tailored to the individual child. Emily's question, and answer, suggests that even at a young age she had strong opinions and a sense of justice. Emily was inclined towards compassion and kindness – she does, after all, suggest reasoning with her brother first – but if that does not work she is more than willing to administer punishment of a stronger kind.

Patrick's line of questioning to Emily hints that she had already had run-ins with Branwell, and had shown her brother that, although he was older, she was not a sister to be messed with. This relationship between the two would continue into adulthood. Although there was real love between Branwell and Emily, it was she who was the dominant force in their relationship.

With six young children sharing the same space day after day, it is natural that friction should occur from time to time, but it is remarkable that the Brontë siblings still seem to have thrived in each other's company, as both children and adults. When we think of Emily, Charlotte and Anne today, it is easy to get the mistaken impression that they were serious, even sullen children, always to be found with their head in a book or working silently away at stories of their own making. While it is certainly true that the young Brontës loved to read, this is only part of the story of their younger days.

Even before they began to write, the Brontës were embracing their creativity in other ways – and their sole objective in this first creative outpouring was fun. Charlotte and Emily were the driving forces behind this, and as they shared a room, the evening hours were often spent inventing and then acting out tales – or plays, as they chose to call them. Charlotte gives an insight into this in a 'History of the Year' that she wrote in 1829:

> Emily's and my bed plays were established the 1st December 1827 ... Bed plays mean secret plays, they are very nice ones. All our plays are very strange ones, their nature I need not write on paper for I think I shall always remember them.[2]

At other times, the sisters would gather together with their brother Branwell to re-enact scenes from history they had read or heard about. One such occasion damaged the only tree in their garden, and posed a risk to Emily's head too. We know from the Brontës' friend, Ellen Nussey, that the garden in front of the parsonage was sparse except for 'a few stunted thorns and shrubs, and a few current bushes which Emily and Anne treasured as their own fruit-garden'.[3] There was, however, one solitary tree which was therefore treasured by Patrick.

The children must have been learning about the English Civil War and its aftermath, as they decided to recreate the flight of the future King Charles II after the Battle of Worcester in 1651. He famously evaded capture by Roundhead troops by hiding in an oak tree all day, and this allowed him to escape from England before returning nine years later to claim the throne and restore the monarchy. Predictably, it was the nature-loving Emily who volunteered to play the part of the king, demonstrating a fearlessness in the face of danger that she would show again in her final days.

Climbing the parsonage's cherry tree, she hid in its branches as her Roundhead sisters and brother paraded below. Alas, a branch broke, sending Emily falling to the ground. Emily's first thought was not for any injury or hurt to herself, but how to conceal the damage to the tree from her father. The children walked to the nearby house of the young sexton, John Brown, who would later become a firm friend of Branwell. Brown was a practical man and agreed to paint the exposed part of the tree revealed by the broken branch in an effort to conceal it. His efforts were in vain, as Patrick soon spotted what had happened, but this incident shows both the Brontë children at play and the kindness with which Haworth villagers such as John Brown viewed them.[4]

Another incident from around this time, at some point in the 1820s, showed how the children's play would sometimes take a mischievous turn. One day they were under the watchful eye of Tabby Aykroyd, a kind and faithful old woman who had been brought into the parsonage in 1824 after Nancy Garrs left to be married. Tabby would remain at the parsonage until she died in 1855, except for a spell when she lived with her sister while she recovered from a leg injury. Tabby and the children had great affection for each other, and she would often tell them folk tales from days gone by, stories that burrowed deep into Emily's mind, and that would later be an influence on *Wuthering Heights*.

On this particular day, the children were playing one of their games, with Tabby presumably doing the housework in the background, but they became so enrapt in their characters that the poor servant became terrified. Branwell's friend and biographer Francis Leyland heard later how Tabby had run to the house of her nephew William, shouting, 'William! William! Yah mun goa up to Mr Brontë's for aw'm sure yon chiller's all gooin mad, and I dar'nt stop ith house ony longer wi'em; and aw'll stay here woll yah come back!'[5] When William Wood neared the parsonage, he was greeted by a great hooting of laughter, with Emily and her sisters and brother delighting at how effective their play had been.

These incidents give us an insight into the lives of the young Brontës when they were together. They were children very much like those of today, not solely serious or gloomy, as some would imagine, but rather children who loved to play and laugh together, who could be mischievous as well as kind and obedient. The early death of their mother, and the deaths of Maria and Elizabeth Brontë just a few years later, must have been a catalyst for the close bonds that formed between them. In learning to become self-sufficient at an early age, however, they also became wary of people unknown. This is especially true in Emily's case, so that her personality eventually had two distinct sides to it: forthright and powerful in the presence of her siblings, yet painfully quiet and shy in the company of others.

Patrick Brontë, although essentially a rather insular man himself, would by necessity often have visitors at the parsonage for parish-related matters, and these visits by strangers, or half-strangers, could prove very trying for Emily. She, often with Anne alongside her, would frequently hide in her room, or even under tables or behind curtains when visitors arrived. These incidents could have been the inspiration for the opening of Charlotte's great novel *Jane Eyre*, with the young Jane taking refuge behind a curtain as she reads a book.

It should be noted, however, that this extreme shyness was not confined to Emily and Anne, nor even to their childhood years. Elizabeth Gaskell records one such incident that affected Charlotte Brontë in April 1853:

One evening we had, among other guests, two sisters who sang Scottish ballads exquisitely. Miss Brontë had been sitting quiet and constrained till they began 'The Bonnie House of Airlie', but the effect of that and 'Carlisle Yetts', which followed, was as irresistible as the playing of the Piper of Hamelin.

The beautiful clear light came into her eyes; her lips quivered with emotion; she forgot herself, rose, and crossed the room to the piano, where she asked eagerly for song after song. The sisters begged her to come and see them the next morning, when they would sing as long as ever she liked; and she promised gladly and thankfully. But on reaching the house her courage failed. We walked some time up and down the street; she upbraiding herself all the while for folly, and trying to dwell on the sweet echoes in her memory rather than on the thought of a third sister who would have to be faced if we went in. But it was of no use; and dreading lest this struggle with herself might bring on one of her trying headaches, I entered at last and made the best apology I could for her non-appearance.[6]

When the oppression of strangers or life spent within the parsonage became too much, there was one place more than any other that Emily Brontë longed to fly – the moors. Emily's passion for the bleak beauty of Haworth Moors is well known, and it was a love that had its roots in her infancy.

Patrick was himself a keen walker and a believer in the health-giving qualities of fresh air. It was for this reason that he encouraged his children to walk on the moors that tumbled away from their parsonage home. In their early days, Nancy or Sarah Garrs would lead these expeditions, although Nancy recalled how the kind and practical Elizabeth Brontë would also take the lead, holding onto her younger sisters' hands and taking 'thoughtful care' of them.[7] Was Emily's later adoption of the pen name 'Ellis' a tribute to her tragic sister Elizabeth who had been kind to her as a young girl? It could also be that Elizabeth is present in the character of the housekeeper Zillah in *Wuthering Heights*, Zillah being an antiquated shortened form of Elizabeth.

Elizabeth Brontë was absent on one particular walk, as were Maria and Charlotte, all of whom were away at Cowan Bridge School. It was in the days before Emily was sent in their footsteps, a time that saw her continue her moorland walks with a young Anne by her side, cementing their growing sisterly friendship. On 2 September 1824, the rains that had been hammering on the parsonage window panes came at last to a halt. It was a moment of rejoicing, for the young Emily and Anne especially, as they loved nothing better than being outside on the moor, and the fresh scent that filled the air after a storm was a heady delight to them. Added to the bad weather of the last few days, a cold had also kept the girls indoors, but they now begged their father to be allowed onto the moors. He readily acquiesced and the Garrs sisters led the way, with Branwell, Emily and Anne following behind.

After walking for around 2 miles, which must have been about the limit for young Anne at the time, the weather and light changed without warning. The sky darkened with a strange suddenness and an ominous rumble carried across the moors. The earth shook violently, and then large hailstones fell from the sky. It had now become very dark, and Nancy and Sarah realised that something was dreadfully wrong. In the distance was the large Ponden Hall and, gathering the children up, they ran towards it, with a voice from within the hall urging them on. They had just reached the shelter of a porch when a huge torrent of water and mud flooded across the landscape they had been walking in. This was Emily's first encounter with Ponden Hall, but it was one that she would not forget. It was a building she would come to know well in coming years, and although Top Withens marks the isolated moorland location of Wuthering Heights, it is Ponden Hall that supplied many of the details of the building itself.

At the peak of its fury, the torrent picked up boulders and carried them down to the moors (the devastation can still be seen on the scarred and cratered moors today), and the sound of an apparent explosion was reported as far away as Leeds. For weeks afterwards, the streams were full of dead fish.

Patrick Brontë had known something was wrong, and had watched from a window of the parsonage with a sense of dread as the sky above turned black, transforming daytime into an instant night. Patrick preached a sermon about the event on 12 September, and we have a record of his words on this emotional occasion:

> I had sent my little children, who were indisposed, accompanied by the servants, to take an airing on the common, and as they stayed rather longer than I expected, I went to an upper chamber to look for their return. The heavens over the moors were blackening fast. I heard muttering of distant thunder, and saw the frequent flashing of the lightning ... My little family had escaped to a place of shelter, but I did not know it. I consequently watched every movement of the coming tempest with a painful degree of interest. The house was perfectly still. Under these circumstances, I heard a deep, distant explosion.[8]

Patrick could wait no longer, and oblivious to the very real danger to himself, he set out immediately, walking through the storm and the deluge of mud until he found his children. A relative of Sarah Garrs later revealed the story she heard about what happened next: 'They [the Brontë children] were frightened, and hid themselves under Sarah's cloak, and Mr Brontë went in search of them and found them in a porch ... terrified, and so was he till he found them.'[9]

It was widely believed at the time that an earthquake had occurred, but in fact it was a rare event that has become known as the Crow Hill bog burst. Constant rain had eroded the soil until a landslip occurred, and the accumulation of water under the surface gathered force and momentum until mud and water broke free with explosive force. The *Leeds Mercury* reported how the tsunami of mud had reached 7ft high, and revealed how lucky Emily Brontë and her walking companions were: 'Somebody gave alarm, and thereby saved the lives of some children who would otherwise have been swept away.'[10]

This close encounter with death may well have terrified Anne and Branwell, and understandably so, but from what we know of Emily's character it is unlikely to have had the same impact on her. Once safe, she would have gazed wide-eyed with awe at what was happening around her. This was nature at its strongest and most deadly, and also at its most majestic and beautiful. What had been still and silent held an unstoppable power within it and once unleashed it could not be halted, sweeping away everything before it. The mundane had become the magical, but it was a magic that could be neither understood nor tamed. It was an image of what Emily Brontë herself would become.

4

SWEET, TRUSTFUL
CHILD!

The winter wind is loud and wild,
Come close to me, my darling child;
Forsake thy books, and mateless play;
And, while the night is gathering grey,
We'll talk its pensive hours away;—
Ierne, round our sheltered hall
November's gusts unheeded call;
Not one faint breath can enter here
Enough to wave my daughter's hair,
And I am glad to watch the blaze
Glance from her eyes, with mimic rays;
To feel her cheek so softly pressed,
In happy quiet on my breast.
But, yet, even this tranquillity
Brings bitter, restless thoughts to me;
And, in the red fire's cheerful glow,
I think of deep glens, blocked with snow;
I dream of moor, and misty hill,
Where evening closes dark and chill;

For, lone, among the mountains cold,
Lie those that I have loved of old.
And my heart aches, in hopeless pain
Exhausted with repinings vain,
That I shall greet them ne'er again!
Father, in early infancy,
When you were far beyond the sea,
Such thoughts were tyrants over me!
I often sat, for hours together,
Through the long nights of angry weather,
Raised on my pillow, to descry
The dim moon struggling in the sky;
Or, with strained ear, to catch the shock,
Of rock with wave, and wave with rock;
So would I fearful vigil keep,
And, all for listening, never sleep.
But this world's life has much to dread,
Not so, my Father, with the dead.
Oh! not for them, should we despair,
The grave is drear, but they are not there;
Their dust is mingled with the sod,
Their happy souls are gone to God!
You told me this, and yet you sigh,
And murmur that your friends must die.
Ah! my dear father, tell me why?
For, if your former words were true,
How useless would such sorrow be;
As wise, to mourn the seed which grew
Unnoticed on its parent tree,
Because it fell in fertile earth,
And sprang up to a glorious birth –
Struck deep its root, and lifted high
Its green boughs, in the breezy sky.
But, I'll not fear, I will not weep

For those whose bodies rest in sleep, –
I know there is a blessed shore,
Opening its ports for me, and mine;
And, gazing Time's wide waters o'er,
I weary for that land divine,
Where we were born, where you and I
Shall meet our Dearest, when we die;
From suffering and corruption free,
Restored into the Deity.
Well hast thou spoken, sweet, trustful child!
And wiser than thy sire;
And worldly tempests, raging wild,
Shall strengthen thy desire –
Thy fervent hope, through storm and foam,
Through wind and ocean's roar,
To reach, at last, the eternal home,
The steadfast, changeless, shore!

('Faith and Despondency', dated 6 November 1844)

CHARLOTTE BRONTË WAS a brilliant observer of human nature in her novels, of course, but she was a rather less reliable witness when it came to her own family. Her own thoughts and weaknesses sometimes clouded her judgement of the actions of those around her. One example of this is the statement she made in a letter to W.S. Williams, one of her publishers, after the death of her brother Branwell in 1848:

> My poor father naturally thought more of his only son than of his daughters, and much and long has he suffered on his account – he cried out for his loss like David for that of Absalom – My son! My son! And refused at first to be comforted.[1]

Charlotte, desperately saddened by the loss of her only brother and eaten by guilt at the rift that had grown between them in the preceding years, was completely wrong to say that her father thought more of his son than his daughters; but there was one child whom Patrick Brontë was particularly close to and proud of – his daughter, Emily.

The world in which Emily and her siblings grew up was a patriarchal one. It was commonly believed that men were born to be breadwinners, whereas women would be the housekeepers or housewives. It was this attitude that the Brontës had to fight against when trying to make their way in literature, leading them to adopt male pseudonyms in an attempt to overcome the widely held prejudices of the day.

As the daughters of a Church of England priest, the Brontë sisters held a perfectly respectable place in society, yet their father was far from wealthy and had no independent means, as many men of the cloth had at this time. This put the Brontë family firmly into the lower middle-class bracket, in a period when social mobility was much harder to achieve than it is today. It is for this reason that the girls would have been expected to take on one of the two occupations that were suitable for women of their background – governess or teacher. From an early age, however, they had rather different ambitions: they dreamt of being writers.

It was this dream that led Emily, Charlotte, Anne and Branwell to spend long childhood hours around their dining table writing stories and poems, and they were not afraid to ask some of the greatest literary names of their day for their opinion. One infamous example of this came when Charlotte Brontë sent some of her verse to the Poet Laureate, William Southey, and asked for his views on them. Unfortunately, we lack Charlotte's original letter of 29 December 1836, sent when she was 20 years old, but we have Southey's reply.

He begins by apologising for a three-month delay in responding, owing to his travels around the country. He then says that he suspects the writer has used a fictitious signature, which is slightly ironic given what we later know about the Brontës' guise as the Bell brothers, as Charlotte had actually used her real name on this occasion. Southey then goes on to say, 'You evidently possess & in no inconsiderable degree what Wordsworth calls "the faculty of verse".'[2] Southey then makes a pronouncement that, while made with sincerity, seems laughable at best today:

> There is a danger of which I would with all kindness & earnestness warn you. The daydreams in which you habitually indulge are likely to induce a distempered state of mind, & in proportion as all the 'ordinary uses of the world' seem to you 'flat & unprofitable', you will be unfitted for them, without becoming fitted for anything else. Literature cannot be the business of a woman's life: & it ought not to be. The more she is engaged in her proper duties, the less leisure she will have for it, even as an accomplishment & a recreation. To those duties you have not yet been called, & when you are you will be less eager for celebrity. You will not then seek in imagination for excitement.[3]

Thankfully, few people today would agree with Southey's comments, but perhaps surprisingly Charlotte was elated by them. She wrote back to the Poet Laureate, thanking him for his letter which was 'so considerate in its tone, so noble in spirit'.[4] Charlotte also kept the letter in its original envelope, upon which she wrote, 'Southey's advice. To be kept forever.'[5]

We can imagine Charlotte gleefully reading the letter to Emily, and Emily may have kept her counsel to preserve her sister's feelings, but she is unlikely to have been as impressed. Southey was, however, simply espousing the beliefs of the day – a woman's aim in life was to marry, and once she had done that she would have all the excitement she needed in the form of cooking, washing and looking after the house. Thankfully, it was not a view that Patrick Brontë concurred with.

Patrick was a firm believer in the transformative power of education – it had, after all, given him a very different life to the one he could have expected in County Down. He saw it not only as a means of attaining skills and knowledge for the workplace, but as something to be treasured in its own right. This was revolutionary thinking at a time when children, especially children from poorer backgrounds, were seen as little more than mini-adults and put to work as soon as possible. Even more unusually, compared to the general thinking of his time, Patrick believed that education and the acquisition of knowledge was important for girls as well as boys. It was this attitude that encouraged Emily Brontë's creativity and allowed her imagination to take flight. Emily was permitted uncensored access to books, newspapers and magazines from an early age.

Most middle-class parents of the time would have kept a close eye on what their daughters were reading. In fact, reading as a whole was considered less important than learning skills deemed more feminine and useful; skills such as needlework, art and music, that would form the basis of the lessons that Emily and her sisters would themselves give in their time as governesses and teachers. Patrick, however, was a keen reader himself, and was delighted to see that his children seemed to be following his lead. He not only allowed them access to periodicals and newspapers, from the *Leeds Intelligencer* to the patriotic *John Bull*, he also let them choose whatever they wanted from his own library.

As a child, Emily was particularly fascinated by *Tales from the Arabian Knights, Aesop's Fables* and the eighteenth-century collection *Tales of the Genii* by Sir Charles Morrell. Morrell was British Ambassador at Bombay and, in his book, he translated ancient Persian poems by a man named Horam. This is what the Brontës believed, and what the author wanted his readers to believe, but in fact it was all a lie. Morrell was actually the pseudonym of an army chaplain named James Ridley, and all the stories came from nowhere other than his imagination. It was an example that Emily was to follow, conjuring up her own tales and poems behind the protection of a pen name.

As they grew up, the Brontës found a wide range of reading materials to choose from, including works by the likes of Lord Byron and the atheist Percy Shelley, which most fathers of the time would not have dreamt of letting their daughters near. An indication of the books available to Emily in her childhood is given in a letter that Charlotte Brontë wrote to Ellen Nussey in 1834. In it, she gives advice on what to read and what to leave alone (some of which we may find surprising), and we can imagine Charlotte giving similar advice to her younger sisters, Emily and Anne:

If you like poetry let it be first rate, Milton, Shakespeare, Thomson, Goldsmith, Pope (if you will though I don't admire him), Scott, Byron, Campbell, Wordsworth and Southey. Now Ellen don't be startled at the names of Shakespeare, and Byron. Both these were great men and their works are like themselves. You will know how to choose the good and avoid the evil, the finest passages are always the purest, the bad are invariably revolting you will never wish to read them over twice. Omit the comedies of Shakespeare and the Don Juan, perhaps the Cain of Byron though the latter is a magnificent poem.[6]

If Charlotte did pass on this advice to Emily, it was unlikely to have been heeded. As a girl and a woman, Emily would not be told what to do and what not to do, although she would have been in complete agreement with another recommendation later in Charlotte's letter to Ellen: 'For fiction – read Scott alone, all novels after his are worthless.'[7]

Walter Scott became beloved of all three writing sisters, and they were introduced to his work at an early age, thanks to a thoughtful present from their Aunt Branwell. At Christmas 1828 she gifted them Scott's new book, *Tales of a Grandfather*. It is a book designed to make the history of Scotland accessible to younger readers, and it captivated Charlotte, Branwell, Emily and Anne. The love of Scott can be seen most clearly, however, in Emily's writing, both in the landscapes of her poetry and especially in *Wuthering Heights*, which is clearly influenced by his novel *The Bride of Lammermoor*.

There was another writer of prose and poetry who surely influenced Emily: her own father. Patrick was a keen if not always accomplished writer throughout his life. While, in later years, this took the form of sermons and letters to local newspapers, in his earlier days Patrick Brontë was a published writer of prose and poetry. His first foray into print came in 1811, when he published a collection of poetry entitled *Cottage Poems*. This collection consisted of a dozen poems that were written, in Patrick's own words, 'for the unlearned and the poor'.[8] In 1813 he followed this with another collection of verse entitled *The Rural Minstrel*, which is clearly influenced by his love for his new wife, Maria. One poem, *Kirkstall Abbey*, describes the once great but now ruined monastery near Leeds, and the site at which Patrick proposed to Maria Branwell.[9]

Patrick's poetry, to my mind, shares traits in common with Charlotte Brontë's, in that while the poems are carefully worded they are also frequently over long and over dramatised. Perhaps mindful of this, Patrick next turned his attention to prose. In 1818, the year of Emily's birth, the company of Baldwin, Cradock & Joy published his only novel. By its title we can tell that he did not altogether lose his florid style in the transition from poetry to prose: *The Maid of Killarney; or Albion and Flora; a Modern Tale; in which are Interwoven Some Cursory Remarks on Religion and Politics.*

The Maid of Killarney tells the story of an Englishman named Albion, who wanders alone in Ireland until he falls in love with a local girl named Flora. He later converts to Christianity and marries the girl. The book is as much a political allegory as anything else, looking at the political unrest that was rife in the north of Ireland at the time, and the divide that existed between Protestants and Catholics. While it is doubtful that Emily found *The Maid of Killarney* as exciting as *The Bride of Lammermoor*, it would surely have given her a thrill to see her father's book on their bookshelves, and this physical example of the Brontë family in print would have encouraged her and her sisters in their later endeavours. Reading her father's prose and poetry also revealed to Emily a kindred spirit.

Patrick Brontë's writing is often of a didactic nature, but it also reveals his love of nature, as in his poem 'The Rainbow', which includes lines such as:

Ever blessed be those innocent days,
Ever sweet their remembrance to me;
When, often, in silent amaze,
Enraptured, I'd gaze upon thee!
Whilst arching a-down the black sky,
Thy colours glowed on the green hill,
To catch thee, as lighting I'd fly,
But, aye, you eluded my skill.[10]

There is evidence in his verse of Patrick's love of the more wilder and more powerful side of nature – something which thrilled Emily more than anything else.

There also survives a handful of tender and moving letters from Maria Branwell to Patrick Brontë during their rapid courtship. In one letter, she refers to Patrick's previous correspondence in which he had imagined a shipwreck: 'I really know not what to make of the beginning of your last; the winds, waves and rocks almost stunned me. I thought you were giving me the account of some terrible dream.'[11] Patrick could conjure up thunderstorms and typhoons from his own imagination, just as Emily would in her poems and novel, and this is one of the factors that drew them increasingly closer together.

When Emily was a child, Patrick would have been delighted at her intellect, the young promise noted when she entered Cowan Bridge School. As she grew older, however, he learned to appreciate her mature qualities even more. Here was a shy woman with a great mind, and yet one who delighted in domestic duties and aspects of everyday life that some would find mundane. She loved to read and write at every opportunity, and of course she loved being at one with nature – and the wilder the weather, the more she liked it. Patrick could doubtless see some of his tragic wife in Emily, but even more apparent was a reflection of himself, and it was this that made his bond with Emily closer than with any of his other children.

Life as a minister in the busy parish of Haworth often left Patrick with little time for anything other than church work, so his favourite mode of relaxation was walking. Elizabeth Gaskell noted, 'He was an active walker, stretching away over the moors for many miles, noting in his mind all natural signs of wind and weather, and keenly observing all the wild creatures that came and went in the loneliest sweeps of the hills.'[12] Change the 'he' to 'she', and 'his' to 'her', and word for word this could also be a description of Emily Brontë.

When the occasion permitted they would have walked together, and as Emily's reserved nature meant that she spent more time in Haworth than her sisters, it is likely that she enjoyed more walks with her father than any of her siblings. On these walks, and in interludes spent in her father's study, she discussed many subjects with Patrick but, as Emily's poem reveals, one of particular interest was faith and spirituality. We shall see later how Emily gradually abandoned the traditional practices of the Church of England, but she always retained a strong belief in a divine power.

In 'Faith and Despondency', we get more than a hint of the real-life father and daughter conversations. Ierne is a girl of Gondal, reminding her father of the belief that he has instilled in her, and yet tempering it with her own thoughts on the matter. Even though Emily's views on religion did not always align with his own, Patrick would have enjoyed these philosophical debates with his daughter.

Perhaps most of all, Patrick was impressed by his daughter's bravery and her sense of duty. He knew that even though Emily struggled against overwhelming shyness, when she put her mind to something she was sure to do it. He also knew that she would do anything to help those she loved, and it is this quality that led Patrick to hand Emily a very important role that would not necessarily be expected of a young woman.

The early nineteenth century was a dangerous time in the north of England, where the Luddite uprisings were quickly followed by Chartist unrest. Growing divisions within the Church also made the Church of England unpopular with many parishioners across the country as, even if they were Dissenters who did not attend Anglican services, they were still legally bound to pay dues to the official Church.

Patrick, while broadly liked in the Haworth area, was old and wise enough to know that trouble could arise at any moment, and for this reason he kept a shotgun that he loaded at night and then discharged into the air in the morning (this being the only way to empty the weapon). As he grew older, Patrick realised that he should teach one of his children how to shoot as well, in case an attack came when he was away or too old to defend himself and his family. Branwell would seem the obvious choice, but Patrick knew that his increasingly erratic son could not be trusted with a weapon. His pragmatic, and excellent, choice is sweetly summed up in a remembrance from John Greenwood, the village stationer, who was a close friend of the family:

> Patrick had such unbounded confidence in his daughter Emily that he resolved to learn her to shoot too. They used to practice with pistols. Let her be ever so busy in her domestic duties, whether in the kitchen baking bread at which she had such a dainty hand, or at her studies, rapt in a world of her own creating – it mattered not; if he called upon her to take a lesson, she would put all down. His tender and affectionate 'Now, my dear girl, let me see how well you can shoot today', was irresistible to her filial nature and her most winning and musical voice would be heard to ring through the house in response, 'Yes, papa' and away she would run with such a hearty good will taking the board from him, and tripping like a fairy to the bottom of the garden, putting it in its proper position, then returning to her dear revered parent, take the pistol which he had primed and loaded for her. 'Now my girl' he would say, 'take time, be steady'. 'Yes papa' she would say taking the weapon with as firm a hand, and as steady an eye as any veteran of the camp, and fire. Then she would run to fetch the board for him to see how she had succeeded. And she did get so proficient, that she was rarely far from the mark. His 'how cleverly you have done, my dear girl', was all she cared for. 'Oh!' He would exclaim, 'she is a brave and noble girl. She is my right-hand, nay the very apple of my eye!'[13]

Here, in his own words, is the rebuttal to Charlotte's claim that Patrick Brontë thought more of his son than his daughters. Emily, brave, noble and a kindred spirit, was the apple of Patrick's eye. It was a mutual appreciation, and the close bond with her father was one reason that Emily always felt happiest when she was at home in Haworth. There was, however, another member of the Brontë family whom Emily became even closer to.

5

FRIENDSHIP LIKE
THE HOLLY-TREE

Love is like the wild rose-briar,
Friendship like the holly-tree –
The holly is dark when the rose-briar blooms,
But which will bloom most constantly?
The wild rose-briar is sweet in spring,
Its summer blossoms scent the air;
Yet wait till winter comes again,
And who will call the wild-briar fair?
Then scorn the silly rose-wreath now,
And deck thee with the holly's sheen,
That when December blights thy brow,
He still may leave thy garland green.

('Love and Friendship', dated 6 November 1844)

E MILY WAS, FOR the most part, a smiling, happy child, and a resilient one, too, despite the early tragedies that came with the loss of her mother and two elder sisters. Even so, these tragic events did cast a shadow over her life, which increased in size and darkness as she grew older. Those who learned to see past Emily's reserve, such as the stationer John Greenwood, could not help but like the honest, sincere and kind-hearted woman that she became, but she made few close friends throughout her life.

There was, however, one close companion whom Emily would cherish more than anything in the world. She found a soul and heart akin to her own, a person almost as silent as herself, yet they kept no secrets from each other and worked happily by each other's sides throughout their all too brief lives: her younger sister, Anne Brontë.

The Brontë children seemed to turn naturally towards the sibling closest to themselves in age. Maria and Elizabeth were close, until death claimed them both within a few cruel weeks of each other; Charlotte and Branwell were childhood friends and conspirators, until Charlotte spurned her brother in adulthood because of his violent addictions; and finally, we have the last of the Brontë children to be born – Emily and Anne – and, although distance and artistic differences would create temporary separations, their love for each other would remain undiminished.

A first-hand account of this remarkable bond comes from one of the few people outside of the Brontë family to gain Emily's confidence and admiration: a young woman from Birstall, in the West Riding of Yorkshire, called Ellen Nussey. Ellen was a central figure throughout the lives of the Brontë sisters, sending gifts to Emily in her final illness, accompanying Anne on her final journey to Scarborough a few months later,[1] and acting as bridesmaid to Charlotte on her wedding day in 1854. Of equal importance to Brontë lovers today, Ellen is also the source of much of the information we have about the family, thanks to the hundreds of letters from Charlotte Brontë that she preserved for posterity.

Ellen met Charlotte Brontë at Roe Head School, near Mirfield, in January 1831, and a friendship was formed that would be stronger than any other Charlotte would know. Ellen made frequent visits to the Haworth Parsonage throughout the years, and it is her account of her first visit in July 1833 that gives us a glimpse of Emily Brontë at the age of 14, and an indication of her relationship with Anne:

> Emily had by this time acquired a lithesome, graceful figure. She was the tallest person in the house, except her father. Her hair, which was naturally as beautiful as Charlotte's, was in the same unbecoming tight curl and frizz, and there was the same want of complexion. She had very beautiful eyes, kind, kindling, liquid eyes; but she did not often look at you: she was too reserved. She talked very little. She and Anne were like twins – inseparable companions, and in the very closest sympathy, which never had any interruption.[2]

Just what was it that made the relationship between Emily and Anne probably the closest of any within the Brontë household, and undoubtedly the most enduring? The answer lies partly in Emily's character. Her quiet exterior hid a kind and loving persona, one who was always ready and willing to help – whether that meant helping a struggling fledgling found on the moor, or in later years waiting up for her brother to return from an inn so she could guide him up the stairs.

There was a gap of nineteen months between the births of Emily and Anne, the longest period between births in the series of six Brontë children. A bright and precocious child, the young Emily fell instantly in love with the burbling new baby who was being doted upon. She was no longer the youngest in the family, but no hint of jealousy would ever trouble Emily; the role of elder sister was one for which she was ideally suited.

The protective and loving qualities that Emily would become famous for had their first flourishing as she looked down into the crib that already held the most precious thing in the world to her. This sensibility was increased further as the years progressed, because Anne was far from a healthy, robust child. The youngest Brontë sister suffered from asthma, and the wild winds of Haworth Moors would leave her wheezing and gasping for air. At such moments, it is easy to imagine Emily draping a protective arm around her young sister's shoulder. She was there, and would always be there. As Ellen Nussey remembered, 'She and gentle Anne were often seen twined together as united statues of power and humility – they were to be seen with their arms lacing each other in their younger days whenever their occupation permitted their union.'[3]

Emily found her affection reciprocated, so that the villagers of Haworth would soon become used to seeing the two young girls walking hand in hand with each other. Even so, although they were very alike in temperament, they certainly did not look like twins. Emily grew to be tall and willowy, second in height only to her father, but Anne would always be short, and while Emily had the dark hair and dark eyes that the other Brontë girls bore, Anne had the appearance of a Cornish Branwell, with lighter hair and violet eyes that sparkled.

Their close sibling bond found its initial outlet in play, with Emily and Anne sharing walks on the moors together whenever possible, as shown in the report of them begging to be let outside on the day of the Crow Hill bog burst.[4] We get further evidence of this from their first diary paper, jointly composed on 24 November 1834, when Emily was 16 and Anne 14.

There are four sets of diary papers currently known to exist, dating from the years 1834, 1837, 1841 and 1845. The first two were composed and signed by Emily and Anne Brontë together, while in the last two years the sisters composed their own separate diary papers. They offer a fascinating glimpse of their everyday lives, their creative endeavours and their often-moving hopes for the future. They also show the development of the sisterly relationship between the two, and provide the most direct insight of all into Emily's character and thoughts. In many ways they are mundane, talking of baking, homework and train rides, but it is a magical mundanity as it takes us into the mind of Emily Brontë, the vicar's daughter, as opposed to the genius writer we all know.

The papers also show the educational and intellectual progress of Emily and Anne, as their first papers are littered with spelling and grammatical errors, although the second one also contains a charming picture of Emily and Anne writing at their table. The diary paper of 1834 reads:

I fed Rainbow, Diamond, Snowflake, Jasper, pheasent this morning Branwell went down to Mr Drivers and brought news that Sir Robert peel was going to stand for Leeds. Anne and I have been peeling apples for Charlotte to make an apple pudding and for Aunts nuts and apples. Charlotte said she made puddings perfectly and she was of a quick but limted intellect. Tabby said just now come Anne pilloputate (i.e. pill a potato) Aunt has come into the kitchen just now and said where are your feet Anne? Anne answered On the floor Aunt. Papa opened the parlour Door and gave Branwell a Letter saying here Branwell read this and show it to your Aunt and Charlotte – The Gondals are discovering the interior of Gaaldine, Sally Mosley is washing in the back kitchin.

It is past twelve o'clock Anne and I have not tided ourselves, done our bed work done our lessons and we want to go out to play. We are going to have for dinner boiled beef, turnips, potato's and apple pudding, the kitchin is in a very untidy state. Anne and I have not Done our music exercise which consists of b major. Tabby said on my putting a pen in her face Ya pitter pottering there instead of pilling a potate, I answered O Dear, O Dear, O Dear, I will directly. With that I get up, take a knife and begin pilling (finished pilling the potatoes) papa going to walk Mr Sunderland expected.

Anne and I say I wonder what we shall be like and what we shall be and where we shall be if all goes on well in the year 1874 – in which year I shall be in my 57th year Anne will be going in her 55th year Branwell will be going in his 58TH year and Charlotte in her 59th year hoping we shall all be well at that time we close our paper.[5]

This is our first real insight into the mind of Emily, and an illuminating one. Ignoring the spelling and punctuation (which would improve greatly by the time she came to set down her poetry), we see Emily taking an interest in politics, with Branwell bringing news that the leading politician and future prime minister, Sir Robert Peel, was going to stand in the nearby constituency of Leeds. We also get a glimpse of Emily's growing infatuation with her imaginary kingdoms of Gondal and Gaaldine, which we shall examine in the next chapter. Most of all, we get an impression of the closeness of the two sisters behind the composition, Emily and Anne. They have homework to do, and have not even tidied themselves or their bedrooms, but all they want to do is go outside and play together on the moors.

As the sisters grew up together, they also developed a love of writing and reading together, and perhaps unsurprisingly they were in accord when it came to matters of literature too. Evidence of this can be found in a great work of literature that is too often overlooked today: Charlotte Brontë's third (although the second to be published) novel *Shirley*.

Shirley, in my opinion, is Charlotte's greatest masterpiece, and yet it is not nearly as lauded as *Jane Eyre* or *Villette*. One reason that I like the novel so much, and why I particularly recommend it to Brontë lovers, is that it contains thinly veiled portraits of many of the people and places Charlotte knew. Thus, we see characters based upon her former headteacher Miss Margaret Wooler, her great friend Mary Taylor, and her future husband Arthur Bell Nicholls. Most important of all, however, are the pen portraits of the novel's two heroines: Shirley Keeldar and Caroline Helstone.

Shirley, as Charlotte admitted to her biographer and friend Elizabeth Gaskell, was based upon Emily Brontë, and it is clear also that Caroline is based upon Anne. When read with this knowledge, it becomes a particularly moving novel. When Charlotte began writing *Shirley* her two sisters were happy and healthy, but by the time she had finished the novel both of them had died of tuberculosis. The novel became a tribute to her loved and lost sisters, and at the heart of the novel is the unbreakable bond that forms between the headstrong Shirley and the kind and gentle Caroline. It is in Charlotte's words that we see the tastes her younger sisters shared in common:

> Caroline's instinct of taste, too, was like her [Shirley's] own. Such books as Miss Keeldar had read with the most pleasure were Miss Helstone's delight also. They held many aversions too in common, and could have the comfort of laughing together over works of false sentimentality and pompous pretension.[6]

At a pivotal point in the novel, Caroline refuses to leave Shirley's side in a moment of danger. This conversation is an echo of the sisters' walks upon the moors when, with Emily's encouragement, Anne would find courage that she would not otherwise possess:

> 'I am a blind, weak fool, and you are acute and sensible, Shirley. I will go with you; I will gladly go with you!'
> 'I do not doubt it. You would die blindly and meekly for me …'
> Caroline rapidly closed shutter and lattice. 'Do not fear that I shall not have breath to run as fast as you can possibly run, Shirley. Take my hand. Let us go straight across the fields.'
> 'But you cannot climb walls?'

'To-night I can.'

'You are afraid of hedges, and the beck which we shall be forced to cross?'

'I can cross it.'[7]

This mutual love of nature and a mutual appreciation of the same things in literature were the foundations of a lasting and loving relationship – the evergreen holly that is always there when we need it. Emily's poem not only lauds the virtues of this kind of relationship, however, it also spurns the charms of the more obviously beautiful wild rose – so, what was her reason for this?

It was written in late 1844, at a time when Anne was away from Emily, thanks to her job as a governess to the Robinson family of Thorp Green Hall, near York. It was also a time when Anne was at one of her lowest ebbs, and although we no longer have the letters, given Anne's love of correspondence,[8] it seems certain that she would have sent despondent letters home to her beloved sister Emily.

The main source of Anne's discontent was the increasingly erratic behaviour of Branwell, for whom Anne had secured a post as governor alongside her. Emily may well have thought, however, that Anne was still being brought low by the memories of the man she had loved – the assistant curate William Weightman. We shall read later of the impact that Weightman had on Emily's life, but after his sudden death from cholera in September 1842, contracted after a visit to a sick parishioner, it was Anne who was hardest hit. She had dreamt of a life together with the kind, dashing churchman, but her hopes and desires now lay under the stone floor of the Haworth church she knew so well.

From the moment of Weightman's death, Anne composed a series of poems of love and mourning that can only be seen as an indication of her feelings for the first, probably only, man she had loved. Emily would have become increasingly concerned by the impact this grief was having on Anne's physical and mental health – an impact that seemed to be growing, rather than diminishing, with the years. It is this that leads to Emily's advice in her poem: look always for friendship that will endure, and prize it over fleeting thoughts of love that can only be transient and leave us feeling empty when they have gone, just as we miss the beauty we once saw in the wild rose briar once it is blighted by winter.

As Ellen Nussey stated in her reminiscence, Emily and Anne remained forever close – and this was reflected in their writing as much as anything else. The kingdom of Gondal, which made up so much of Emily's poetry and that could also be seen reflected in *Wuthering Heights*, was a creation of Emily and Anne alone, and it is fitting that, when Emily's novel was published by Thomas Cautley Newby, it shared a three-volume set with Anne's debut novel, *Agnes Grey*.

Nevertheless, as the girls grew into womanhood, and as the miles separated them during Anne's stints as a governess and during Emily's months at school in Brussels,[9] their relationship inevitably changed. The distance between them could do little to diminish Emily's affection for her sister, however, as we see in her diary paper of 30 July 1841 (Emily's 23rd birthday), written during Anne's time at Thorp Green Hall. Emily begins by entitling her missive 'A paper to be opened when Anne is 25 years old or my next birthday after – if all be well'.[10]

The conclusion of this diary paper reveals how Anne continued to be in Emily's thoughts, however far away she was. 'Now I close by sending from far an exhortation of courage! to exiled and harassed Anne wishing she was here.'[11] It is the 1845 diary papers, however, that give the clearest indication of the contrasting attitudes and emotions of the sisters, by then in their mid-twenties. Emily is still full of vigour and optimism, and she writes gleefully of a journey to York that she and her sister have just taken together:

Anne and I went on our first long journey by ourselves together, leaving home on the 30th of June, Monday sleeping at York – returning to Keighley Tuesday evening sleeping there and walking home on Wednesday morning – though the weather was broken we enjoyed ourselves very much except during a few hours at Bradford and during our excursion we were Ronald Macelgin, Henry Angora, Juliet Angusteena, Rosabelle, Ella and Julian Egramon, Catherine Navarre and Cordelian Fitzaphnold escaping from the palaces of Instruction to join the Royalists who are hard driven at present by the victorious Republicans.[12]

This is a happy tale of the sisters adopting the personas of the Gondal characters they had been creating together since childhood, but it contrasts sharply with the end of Anne's corresponding diary paper:

The Gondals in general are not in first rate playing condition – will they improve? I wonder where we shall all be and where situated on the thirtieth of July 1848 when if we are all alive Emily will be just 30 I shall be in my 29th year Charlotte in her 33rd and Branwell in his 32nd and what changes shall we have seen and known and shall we be much changed ourselves? I hope not – for the worse at least – I for my part cannot well be flatter or older in mind than I am now – Hoping for the best I conclude.[13]

It may seem strange that Anne should wonder whether they would all be alive in July 1848, as at the time she wrote the diary paper they were all in rude health. Of course, when that date did arrive they were all alive, although Charlotte was the only one who would have more than a year to live.

Anne's torpor was a result of many factors, including Branwell's behaviour and religious questions that often played on her mind, but memories of lost love also played their part.

The wild rose wreath had lost its bloom, but Anne would never be completely alone; she always had Emily to turn to. The years to come would bring them both triumph and tragedy, but the one constant was the love that the two sisters had and the support they provided each other. Their relationship did not diminish, it evolved, and would always be there whenever the cold wuthering winds howled across the moors, standing firm like the holly tree itself.

6

THE WORLD WITHIN

When weary with the long day's care,
And earthly change from pain to pain,
And lost, and ready to despair,
Thy kind voice calls me back again:
Oh, my true friend! I am not lone,
While thou canst speak with such a tone!
So hopeless is the world without;
The world within I doubly prize;
Thy world, where guile, and hate, and doubt,
And cold suspicion never rise;
Where thou, and I, and Liberty,
Have undisputed sovereignty.
What matters it, that all around,
Danger, and guilt, and darkness lie,
If but within our bosom's bound,
We hold a bright, untroubled sky,
Warm with ten thousand mingled rays,
Of suns that know no winter days?
Reason, indeed, may oft complain,
For Nature's sad reality,
And tell the suffering heart how vain,

Its cherished dreams must always be;
And Truth may rudely trample down,
The flowers of Fancy, newly-blown:
But thou art ever there, to bring,
The hovering vision back, and breathe,
New glories o'er the blighted spring,
And call a lovelier Life from Death,
And whisper, with a voice divine,
Of real worlds, as bright as thine.
I trust not to thy phantom bliss,
Yet, still, in evening's quiet hour,
With never-failing thankfulness,
I welcome thee, Benignant Power;
Sure solacer of human cares,
And sweeter hope, when hope despairs!

('To Imagination', dated 3 September 1844)

A LOOK AT THE childhood of great writers throughout history can be very revealing as there are often incidents that led inexorably to the creative genius they became. With Emily Brontë, we can pinpoint two such instances which, years later, would result in the creation of *Wuthering Heights*, as well as facilitating the novels of her sisters, Charlotte and Anne. They are moments like others experienced by children, then and now, moments that could have been insignificant but instead changed the course of literary history forever.

We have seen how the Brontës had free and unhindered access to a splendid collection of books as children and adults. They also read contemporary newspapers and periodicals that were passed on to them second-hand by their father, as a teenage Charlotte explained in her 'History of the Year' written in 1829:

> Papa and Branwell are gone for the newspaper the *Leeds Intelligencer* – a most excellent Tory newspaper edited by Mr Wood, the proprietor Mr Hennaman. We take 2 and see 3 Newspapers as such we take the *Leeds Intelligencer* Tory and the *Leeds Mercury* Whig Edited by Mr Bains and his Brother Soninlaw and his 2 sons Edward and Talbot – we see the *John Bull* it is a High Tory very violent.[1]

Putting aside the spelling errors typical of their youthful writing, it is incredible to think that children so young were taking such an interest in politics and newspapers that they knew the names of the editors and proprietors by heart. It was not just the politics of the day that interested the Brontë siblings, however. The early decades of the nineteenth century were a time of conflict, upheaval and exploration, and the tales of real-life adventurers, soldiers and explorers thrilled the Brontës as much as any work of fiction.

The first of two particularly significant items given to the children was contained in the June 1826 edition of *Blackwood's Magazine*. *Blackwood's* was a real treasure trove to Emily and her siblings, as it not only contained lengthy extracts of contemporary fiction, it also featured political debate and the latest news from around the world. This particular issue contained something that instantly grabbed the attention of the eager eyes feasting upon it: an article by a writer called James McQueen, detailing the exploration of central and northern Africa by the explorers Dixon Denham and Hugh Clapperton. Theirs was a fascinating tale, bringing to the attention of readers back in Britain much of the country that we now know as Nigeria. Thankfully, the article glossed over the antipathy between the two men, which saw Denham attempt to besmirch Clapperton's name by having him arrested for theft. Denham was later termed 'the most odious man in the history of geographic discovery'.[2]

To Emily, Charlotte, Anne and Branwell, both Denham and Clapperton were heroes of the fledgling British Empire (taking after their father's example, they were all proud royalists and imperialists). Even more fascinating than the tale of their exploits in *Blackwood's Magazine* was a map accompanying it. The Brontës adored maps of the known world, especially since much of it was changing and being added to on a regular basis. As we shall see, this particular map was put to one side and used again for a very different purpose to the one that concerned Denham and Clapperton.

There was another important event in the month of June 1826 that eventually lead to the Brontë writing we know and love today. It was a Monday evening, 5 June, and Patrick Brontë had just returned to Haworth from Leeds, where he had been on church business. He had bought presents for all of his children, but it was the present for Branwell that has become legendary – a set of twelve wooden soldiers. Here is Charlotte Brontë's account of the event:

Papa bought Branwell some wooden soldiers at Leeds. When Papa came home it was night, and we were in bed, so next morning Branwell came to our door with a box of soldiers. Emily and I jumped out of bed, and I snatched up one and exclaimed: 'This is the Duke of Wellington! This shall be the Duke!' when I had said this Emily likewise took one up and said it should be hers; when Anne came down, she said one should be hers. Mine was the prettiest of the whole, and the tallest, and the most perfect in every part. Emily's was a grave-looking fellow, and we called him 'Gravey'. Anne's was a queer little thing, much like herself, and we called him 'Waiting-boy'. Branwell chose his, and called him Buonaparte.[3]

We have seen reports of Emily from the school at Cowan Bridge and from the Haworth stationer John Greenwood, which paint Emily as cheerful with a pleasant voice and winning personality, but here in Charlotte's words we see another side of her character – now approaching the age of 8, she is already grave and serious at times.

In this one month in June 1826, the Brontës had gained a map that fired their imagination and a set of soldiers that would take their creativity to another level: it was a volcanic combination for minds like theirs. The four children were already adept at making up their own games, whether it was frightening Tabby out of her wits, pretending to be an exiled king, or whispering stories to each other when they should have been sleeping, but now they had a new set of characters to populate their homespun dramas.

The soldiers became known as 'The Twelve' or 'The Young Men', and they were given the names and characters of the people who had become heroes to them. The Duke of Wellington, Arthur Wellesley, and his sons were idolised by Charlotte and so they became her principal characters among The Twelve. Emily and Anne chose the characters of Sir William Parry and Sir James Ross for their soldiers[4] – Arctic explorers who, like the girls, had become inseparable companions.

The first adventure created for The Twelve was later recounted by Branwell in an early composition entitled *The History of the Young Men*. At one point the soldiers, who are lost in the African land of Ashantee, face a terrible monster who captures them and then explains that they are being controlled by immortal and dread beings:

> I am the chief genius Brannii, with me there are 3 others, she, Wellesley, who protects you is named Tallii, she who protects Parry is named Emmii, she who protects Ross is called Annii. Those lesser ones whom ye saw are Genii and Fairies, our slaves and minions. We are the Guardians of this land, we are the guardians of you all.[5]

From the very beginning of the soldiers' adventures, we see the collaborative nature of the Brontë siblings, with Emily, Anne, Charlotte and Branwell taking on the role of overseeing and all-powerful genii of the kind they loved to read about in the *Arabian Nights* stories.

This was far from the end of the soldiers' adventures, however, and in the coming years the tales they inspired would grow exponentially, taking on lives of their own and encompassing stories of love and loss, intrigue and betrayal. For Charlotte and Branwell, it was a childhood fascination that would be put aside once the real world intervened, and for Anne it was something she would turn to occasionally for much-needed escapism from daily drudgery – but for Emily Brontë, it became as important as life itself, with the advancing years only strengthening her reliance on this land of make-believe, this world within.

In this original tale of the young men, the land they conquered, Ashantee, was an amalgamation of many features they had read about in reports of early nineteenth-century exploration. As their storytelling grew more sophisticated and joined up, however, they needed a more permanent base for their adventures: it was then that they returned to the map of Denham and Clapperton's expeditions from *Blackwood's Magazine*. Branwell took the map and made a copy of it, but he replaced the real geographic names with places and features that were now making their first appearances: names such as Sneaky's Land, Parry's Land, Mount Aornos and Wellington's Glass Town.[6]

The young Brontës had created their own fictional world, based upon an actuality that was just being opened up to European eyes. This realm on the western coast of Africa contained regions that were now ruled by each of the children, and at the centre of each region was a great glass town: it became known as the Glass Town Federation, but was later given a new name of Angria.

At first, these adventures in and around the glass towns were played out physically and verbally, but as the children grew older they began to commit their stories to paper, leading to the creation of tiny bound books that can be seen at the Brontë Parsonage Museum, and which have become famous examples of childhood creativity at its finest. The books are made from scraps of paper that have then been stitched together by the girls, underneath a brown paper cover. The writing is so minuscule that it can only be read today with a microscope. This meant that it could not be read by their father, who was very short-sighted, but it also meant it was the perfect size to be read by their toy soldiers.

The inspiration found in *Blackwood's Magazine* was evident, from their appropriation of not only its map but also of its title. With Branwell initially taking charge of the production of the books, they were entitled *Branwell's Blackwoods Magazine*, but after his sister Charlotte took the lead role they were rebranded as *Young Men's Magazine*.

Do not let the size of the books, or magazines, as the Brontës deemed them, nor the age of the four contributors, fool you – they are incredibly sophisticated, full not only of adventure and tragedy but also of humour. The magazines the children read had adverts, so their magazines must have adverts too – but with a sharply satirical twist. For example, one of the earliest editions of *Branwell's Blackwood Magazine*, dated June 1829, finishes with the following advertisement: 'To be sold – 300 Barrels of Prussian Butter & 50 bags of white flour, by Moses ride on the back of an ass'.[7]

The tales of Angria make up a huge body of work for children so young, but they are all written by either Branwell or Charlotte, with their younger siblings Emily and Anne relegated to the background. Their contributions to the stories and magazines were purely verbal ones at this time, but we get an indication of their suggestions when the chief genii Emmii or Annii suddenly appear in a tale, or when their respective heroes Parry or Ross take centre stage.

Emily Brontë was never one to enjoy being kept out of an activity, so she longed to take up her quill and write her own stories – in conjunction with her permanent companion Anne, of course. Their opportunity finally came on 17 January 1831, and it was one they grasped with both hands.

This was the day that Charlotte Brontë returned to formal education after more than five years of home learning, and over five years after the Cowan Bridge tragedy had brought a cessation to the initial schooling of both Charlotte and Emily. The school selected by Patrick on this occasion was very different to the Clergy Daughters' School at Cowan Bridge. Roe Head School, in Mirfield, was run by the kindly Miss Margaret Wooler and, as we shall see, it later welcomed Emily, and then Anne, through its gates.

One immediate effect of Charlotte's removal from Haworth was that it brought to an end the tiny books and magazines about Angria. This could easily have ended the creative adventures of Emily and Anne too, but although undoubtedly missing the presence of her elder sister, Emily also saw the great potential that lay before them. They would leave the confines of Angria, the land that had seen them skulking in the shadows of Mount Aornos, behind, but they would not leave writing behind – it was now time for the youngest Brontës to launch their own kingdom, one that had even more intrigue and complexity – the land of Gondal.

Gondal was a very different country to Angria in many ways. It was not situated in Africa, for a start, but was instead an island kingdom located somewhere in the Pacific Ocean. It was a land full of intrigue and espionage, thanks in part to dynastic struggles that divided families, and thanks also to its conflict with the newly discovered neighbouring island of Gaaldine. We hear of characters plotting against each other, love turning to hate, and there is frequently a dungeon containing a man or woman dreaming of the world they had once known.

It was on this fare that Emily and Anne Brontë truly cut their creative teeth, and we can imagine them discussing plots and counter-plots as they crossed the moors together on their frequent walks. This may be why the landscape of Gondal often resembles the bleak, barren, beautiful moors of Pennine Yorkshire rather than a desert island. An example of this can be found in the very first poem contained within a notebook that Emily headed 'Gondal Poems'. With a date of 6 March 1837, it begins:

There shines the moon, at noon of night –
Vision of glory – Dream of light!
Holy as heaven – undimmed and pure,
Looking down on the lonely moor –
And lonelier still beneath her ray,
That drear moor stretches far away,
Till it seems strange that aught can lie.
Beyond its zone of silver sky – [8]

The tales of Gondal show the incredible imagination and creativity that Emily, particularly, became renowned for, but they also contained echoes of events happening in the real world. An example appears within the second diary paper that Emily and Anne composed together on 26 June 1837: 'Tabby in the kitchin – the Emprerors and Empresses of Gondal and Gaaldine preparing to depart from Gaaldine to Gondal for the coranation which will be on the 12TH of July. Queen Victoria ascended the throne this month.'[9]

The Brontë family, like many across the country, had been captivated by the coronation of the beautiful young Queen Victoria, following the grand build-up in newspapers, both national and local. Emily felt a particular connection to Victoria, as they were born within a year of each other. It was for this reason that the coronation taking place in London was mirrored by a coronation in the Gondalian capital of Regina.

Alas, much of the Gondal writing of both Emily and Anne Brontë has been lost, most likely destroyed before or after their deaths, although we still have many magnificent poems from both the sisters that have their basis in Gondal, yet which often sing of their own feelings and wishes. Most disappointingly, there are no surviving examples of Gondal prose in the manner of the Angrian books and magazines left by Branwell and Charlotte. It is certain, however, that this was a particularly prodigious output. We get a clue to this from Anne Brontë's diary paper of 30 July 1841, in which she writes, 'I am now engaged in writing the 4th volume of Sofala Vernon's life.'[10]

Sofala Vernon was a relatively minor character in the Gondal story when compared to towering figures like the cruel Queen Augusta Geraldine Almeida and the scheming, lustful Julius Brenzaida, and yet Anne was then writing her fourth volume about her. Gondal was a pleasant diversion to Anne, but it was much more to Emily – so we can only begin to imagine how huge Emily's Gondal prose output must have been. It surely contained golden treasures that have been lost to literature forever.

In later years, Anne had posts as governess with the Ingham and Robinson families, while Emily was left at home with her thoughts. It was just what Emily would have wanted, for in this land of her own creation she could shake off her reserved nature and lose herself in a reverie of imagination. These are key reasons why the land of Gondal took such a grip upon Emily: first, she had the time to devote to imagination and creativity in a way that her sisters did not, and second, it gave her a life wildly different to the one she lived within the walls of Haworth's parsonage. To those unaware of her secret, Emily may have sat quietly on her favourite black sofa or silently kneaded bread but, inside her head, tales of love and betrayal, triumph and despair were taking place.

Haworth and Gondal were each as real as the other. Emily and Gondal became so intertwined that she could never extricate herself. She never really tried to. In the final diary paper that we have from Emily, dated 30 July 1845, she writes:

> The Gondals still flourish bright as ever. I am at present writing a work on the First Wars – Anne has been writing some articles on this and a book by Henry Sophona. We intend sticking firm by the rascals as long as they delight us which I am glad to say they do at present.[11]

Emily's Gondal writing fed her imagination and nourished her creative talents. It also gave her an ideal self-education in how to write, and the discipline to do so, even in a house that could be as chaotic as Haworth Parsonage in the latter half of the 1840s. *Wuthering Heights* was Emily's first full novel, but doubtless she had already written many thousands of pages on the heroes and villains of Gondal and Gaaldine.

The poem 'To Imagination' gives us a sense of how important the world of creativity and imagination was to Emily Brontë, but it also gives us a frank insight into her method of creation – one that differs markedly from that of her sisters and most other writers. Emily often felt herself overtaken by an external force when she was writing, as if she was being moved to composition by a power that controlled her as much as she controlled it. This is the 'Benignant Power' that she welcomes in her poem, one that comes to her in the quietness of the evening, a 'hovering vision' that only she can see and feel. It is a striking image that she returns to in many poems, which we will look at in greater detail in Chapter 10. The strange truth is that Emily Brontë was a visionary in more ways than one.

7

SWEET LOVE
OF YOUTH

Cold in the earth—and the deep snow piled above thee,
Far, far removed, cold in the dreary grave!
Have I forgot, my only Love, to love thee,
Severed at last by Time's all-severing wave?
Now, when alone, do my thoughts no longer hover,
Over the mountains, on that northern shore,
Resting their wings where heath and fern-leaves cover,
Thy noble heart forever, ever more?
Cold in the earth—and fifteen wild Decembers,
From those brown hills, have melted into spring:
Faithful, indeed, is the spirit that remembers,
After such years of change and suffering!
Sweet Love of youth, forgive, if I forget thee,
While the world's tide is bearing me along;
Other desires and other hopes beset me,
Hopes which obscure, but cannot do thee wrong!
No later light has lightened up my heaven,
No second morn has ever shone for me;
All my life's bliss from thy dear life was given,

All my life's bliss is in the grave with thee.
But, when the days of golden dreams had perished,
And even Despair was powerless to destroy,
Then did I learn how existence could be cherished,
Strengthened, and fed without the aid of joy.
Then did I check the tears of useless passion –
Weaned my young soul from yearning after thine;
Sternly denied its burning wish to hasten,
Down to that tomb already more than mine.
And, even yet, I dare not let it languish,
Dare not indulge in memory's rapturous pain;
Once drinking deep of that divinest anguish,
How could I seek the empty world again?

('Remembrance', dated 3 March 1845)

THIS POEM, SET in Gondal but, as always, looking at feelings and themes that were very real to Emily, is perhaps her finest love poem. Indeed, some have called it one of the greatest love poems of all time. The exalted twentieth-century literary critic F.R. Leavis commented:

> There is, too, Emily Brontë, who has hardly yet had full justice as a poet; I will record, without offering it as a checked and deliberate critical judgement, that her *Cold in the Earth* is the finest poem in the nineteenth-century part of the *Oxford Book of English Verse.*[1]

Emily Brontë's body of poetry as a whole is complex and diverse, and yet there are themes that keep recurring: death and mourning; religion; the mystical power of poetry and creation; the supremacy of nature; and love, often linked to loss.

This latter theme also played a part in Emily's sole novel, *Wuthering Heights*. It is a story of love, or rather several interconnected stories of love in one book. It shows love in all its forms: passionate, yearning, pure, dark and tortuous, destructive. Heathcliff, on any dispassionate reading, could never be described as an ideal lover. He should surely be seen as the villain of the piece, even if we see some mitigation for his cruelty and obsession, yet he is viewed by many as a romantic hero. Amidst more obvious and family friendly expressions of romantic ardour, from *Pride and Prejudice* to works by Barbara Cartland, it was Emily's *Wuthering Heights* that claimed top spot in a 2007 poll to find the United Kingdom's greatest love story of all time.[2]

Emily Brontë is a woman whose poetry and prose still strikes a chord with lovers of both sexes and all ages so that, to many, she is the archetypal writer of love. Can it be that a woman who knew the nuances of love in all its forms, good and bad, had never experienced romantic love of any kind herself? Sometimes, truth can be stranger than fiction.

Almost since Emily herself, as opposed to the pen name that initially graced her works, first came to the notice of the public, thanks to Charlotte's *Biographical Notice of Ellis Bell*, published two years after her sister's death,[3] people have tried to establish romantic liaisons for her. Some of them have been fanciful, and some of them are with people who never even lived.

In 1936, Virginia Moore penned a book entitled *The Life and Eager Death of Emily Brontë*, in which she used psychological analysis in an attempt to find the true identities of the people in Emily's poetry and prose. As part of her research, she examined at first hand the manuscript of another of Emily's astonishing love poems, *Song by J. Brenzaida to G.S.*, which includes the lines:

> I knew not 'twas so dire a crime,
> To say the word, Adieu:
> But this shall be the only time,
> My slighted heart shall sue ...
> And there are bosoms bound to mine,
> With links both tried and strong;
> And there are eyes whose lightning shine,
> Has warmed and blessed me long:
> Those eyes shall make my only day,
> Shall set my spirit free,
> And chase the foolish thoughts away,
> That mourn your memory![4]

Poring over the tiny writing of this manuscript, Virginia Moore made an astonishing discovery: 'Most arresting and intriguing – the name "Louis Parensell" written above the poem, "I knew not 'twas so dire a crime".'[5]

This was all the proof needed to solve a pressing mystery – how Emily Brontë wrote of love with such understanding if she had never been in love. We now knew that Emily had been in love with a Louis Parensell, and had dedicated one of her greatest love poems to him. Virginia regrets only that there was no diary entry saying 'Emily Brontë loved Louis Parensell'.[6] Of course, there never could be such an entry, as unfortunately Ms Moore had got things entirely wrong.

What she had taken to read 'Louis Parensell' in Emily's handwriting, was actually a pencilled addition to the manuscript in Charlotte Brontë's handwriting. It is a suggested title for the poem, and in fact reads 'Love's Farewell'. Poor Louis never existed but, for a brief moment, he was linked with one of the greatest writers ever to have lived.

Another young man sometimes linked to Emily at least has the advantage of having been a flesh and blood person: Robert Heaton of Ponden Hall. Ponden Hall, or Ponden House as it was known then to distinguish it from the adjacent old hall, would have captured Emily's heart from the moment she first saw it – not only because it offered her protection from the Crow Hill bog burst, but because of the association that brought with it the magical power of nature. In later years, she would become enamoured of its architectural beauty too. Dating originally from Tudor or Elizabethan times, it was extensively rebuilt in 1801, and a stone bearing this date was positioned above the porticoed entrance to the house. It is a feature that would be remembered when Emily came to write *Wuthering Heights*, and explains the dating given at the start of her novel.

The Heatons had been masters of Ponden Hall since the sixteenth century, and this placed them as the leading figures in Haworth and the surrounding district. The head of the family during Emily's time was Robert Heaton, who had married Alice Midgeley,[7] daughter of another prestigious local family who lived at the Manor House (now an inn called Haworth Old Hall). Their exalted position in Haworth society meant that the head of the household was always a trustee at St Michael & All Angels Church, so Robert would have had frequent dealings with the minister at the church, Patrick Brontë.

At times when messages needed to be conveyed to Ponden Hall, Patrick found a willing volunteer in his daughter Emily. She welcomed any opportunity for a moorland walk, and she and Anne especially loved a spot almost halfway to the hall that they called 'the meeting of the waters'.[8] It is here that they often sat and talked about their writing, plotting what terrible event would next befall the inhabitants of Gondal. A stone at this location has become known as the 'Brontë seat', and it has been worn away by people sitting on it over the years, decades and centuries.

Another reason that Emily loved visiting Ponden Hall is that it was home to the thing she loved most – it was not a boy, it was a collection of books. Ponden Hall had a huge library, estimated to be one of the largest private collections of literature in Europe at the time. Among its treasures were many rare works from the eighteenth century, as well as a first folio edition of the plays of William Shakespeare. Emily could still charm people when she wanted to, just as she had at the Clergy Daughters' School, and Robert Heaton let Emily borrow books at will from his collection. It is also said that he planted a pear tree in the garden especially for her.[9]

At the hall, Emily would hear tales of the ghosts and apparitions that were said to haunt it. One was a devil dog known as a gytrash, and another was the grey figure of a man that sometimes appeared in the garden, often headless – if you were unfortunate enough to catch a glimpse of him, it meant a death in the family within a year. These stories were told at Ponden Hall from generation to generation, and Emily must have thrilled at them – indeed, I was told the ghostly stories myself by the current owners, Stephen and Julie, who have now transformed the hall into a prizewinning and rather elegant B&B. They also told me a tale of how Emily was in the hall when one of the family dogs gave birth to a litter of puppies. Emily was completely unfazed at the development, but one young man looking across at her blushed profusely at this demonstration of nature in action. This was the eldest son in the Heaton family, also called Robert, and it is he who is often championed as a potential beau of Emily Brontë.

It is possible that young Robert Heaton was attracted to Emily. We have seen how she could charm those around her, and we have heard reports of her lithesome, graceful figure and beautiful eyes, but it seems less likely that she would have been attracted to him. Robert was four years younger than Emily, and there is no mention of him in her diary papers or allusions to him in her poetry. Could it be, however, that Robert is featured in Emily's great novel – R. Heaton is, after all, an anagram of Hareton? It is an intriguing question, but there would seem to be little to link Hareton as we first see him in *Wuthering Heights*, ill educated and savage, with the privileged eldest son of a wealthy family.

Robert Heaton junior was an admirer from afar, one whom Emily saw when collecting books from the Ponden Hall library, but one who was little noticed or heeded. In fact, we have nothing other than rumours to say whether Robert liked Emily at all, but we know for certain who sent Emily Brontë her first Valentine's card. It was a dashing, kind and well-educated man who, for a few brief years, would brighten up Haworth Parsonage – William Weightman.

Weightman arrived in Haworth in August 1839. He was 25 years old, a native of Appleby, Westmorland, and a graduate of Durham University which, just two years earlier, had become only the third university in England after Oxford and Cambridge. He was taking his first role in what promised to be a glittering ecclesiastical career as assistant curate to Patrick Brontë.

Weightman was the second of six assistant curates who would serve under Reverend Brontë, but he seems to have been the only one whom Patrick ever truly admired (including the sixth and final assistant curate, Arthur Bell Nicholls, who roused his fury by daring to marry his daughter Charlotte). First impressions counted with the normally reserved Brontë sisters, but it says a lot for his character and natural charm that he won them all over from the moment he first met them – including Emily, who would often remain silent when confronted by those she did not know.

As 14 February 1840 approached, Weightman discovered that the three sisters at the parsonage had never received a Valentine's Day card, a tradition that stretched back to the fifteenth century and which far pre-dated the Christmas cards that first appeared in Queen Victoria's reign. We can imagine the delight on the faces of Emily, Anne and Charlotte on the day itself when four cards arrived in the post (one had also been delivered for Ellen Nussey, who was a visitor at the parsonage at the time). The cards were anonymous and had been posted from Bradford; each had a handwritten poem inside tailored to the individual.

Eventually the truth was discovered: the cards were from their father's assistant curate, and he had walked to Bradford to post them, through what must have been treacherous winter conditions, so that the postmark would not give his identity away. It was a kind and thoughtful act of the type for which he would become known within the parish.

Thanks to a letter from Charlotte,[10] we know the titles of three of the four poems that he penned for the sisters and their friend: 'Fair Ellen, Fair Ellen', 'Away Fond Love' and 'Soul Divine'; alas, the fourth poem's name remains a mystery. We can, of course, be safe in attributing the first poem to Ellen Nussey, but which of the other two, if either, was written for Emily? 'Away Fond Love' may have been intended for Anne, who was at that time looking for another post as a governess that would take her away from Haworth (having recently left her post as governess to the Ingham family of Mirfield). 'Soul Divine' may be a suitable title for a poem dedicated to Emily, a woman who was far from humdrum in her thoughts and actions. That would mean that Charlotte failed to mention the title of her own poem, which I think is highly likely as it was almost sacred to her at the time.

We also know the effect that Weightman had on two of the Brontë girls: Charlotte and Anne. Charlotte loved strong, confident, handsome men, and so her head was turned by William Weightman. She writes frequently to Ellen about him, speaking of him in glowing terms, and is teased for spending so long drawing his portrait. By February 1841, however, things have changed. Once again, he sends the Brontë girls a Valentine's Day card, but on this occasion Charlotte writes:

> I got a precious specimen a few days before I left home, but I knew better how to treat it than I did those we received a year ago. I am up to the dodges and artifices of his Lordship's character, he knows I know him ... for all the tricks, wiles and insincerities of love the gentleman has not his match for 20 miles round. He would fain persuade every woman under 30 whom he sees that he is desperately in love with her.[11]

Charlotte has fallen in love with Weightman, but discovered that he cannot love her back – his heart belongs to someone else. There is intense speculation today that this could have been someone whom Charlotte would have seen as the worst possible usurper – her youngest sister, Anne.

We hear of Weightman sitting in church looking sideways at Anne and sighing, while she keeps her eyes downcast. The clearest evidence comes from Anne's writing after Weightman's death. (He died suddenly in September 1842 after contracting cholera from a parishioner he was visiting.) From that moment on, Anne writes a string of poems of mourning and loss with lines such as, 'I will not mourn thee, lovely one, though thou art torn away', 'Yes thou art gone! And never more thy sunny smile shall gladden me', and 'Oh, they have robbed me of the hope my spirit held so dear'. Perhaps the greatest tribute of all comes in *Agnes Grey*, when the title character, clearly based largely upon Anne Brontë herself, falls in love with a kindly assistant curate called Weston and after a separation marries him. It is Anne giving herself the ending in fiction that she had longed for in real life, the ending that death had snatched away from her.

It is clear to me that both Charlotte and Anne Brontë loved William Weightman to some degree, but did he capture Emily's heart too? It seems that she did appreciate his charms, or she would have treated him with the indifference she showed to most people outside of her family. It is certain, however, that Anne would have confided in Emily about her own feelings for Weightman, and this would have been more than enough to ensure that Emily would not get in her way.

Emily liked William Weightman, indeed it seems he was universally liked by all who knew him, as the fulsome funeral oratory by Patrick Brontë and the grand plaque put up in his honour by the Haworth parishioners shows, but she did not love him. While it cannot be ruled out that Emily had a romantic liaison during her only time away from all members of her family, as a teacher in Halifax, it seems almost certain that Emily never knew love for a man: her only loves were the moors, her writing and her sister Anne, and these were more than enough to sustain her through all the days of her life.

Emily never felt the grief that Anne did after the loss of William Weightman, and yet her poems of mourning, especially the one at the head of this chapter, are even more powerful than her sister's. Just as she did with her novel, Emily took source material and turned it into something greater. She felt that 'divinest anguish' only in her mind but, to her, things felt in the mind were just as real as those felt in the external world. She discovered love through literature, and the observation of others, including her sisters and brother, and somehow she then understood and conveyed it better than any of them. Her powers of observation and empathy are almost unparalleled. Charlotte described this unique ability of Emily well in her 1850 preface to *Wuthering Heights*:

My sister's disposition was not naturally gregarious; circumstances favoured and fostered her tendency to seclusion; except to go to church or take a walk on the hills, she rarely crossed the threshold of home. Though her feeling for the people round was benevolent, intercourse with them she never sought; nor, with very few exceptions, ever experienced. And yet she knew them.[12]

It is the same impression we get when reading Emily's poetry and prose today: she knows us.

8

A TYRANT SPELL

The night is darkening round me,
The wild winds coldly blow;
But a tyrant spell has bound me,
And I cannot, cannot go.
The giant trees are bending,
Their bare boughs weighed with snow;
And the storm is fast descending,
And yet I cannot go.
Clouds beyond clouds above me,
Wastes beyond wastes below;
But nothing drear can move me;
I will not cannot go.

('The Night is Darkening Round Me', dated November 1837)

THROUGHOUT EMILY BRONTË's life, the actions of her sisters often had a direct impact upon her. Charlotte's 'accidental discovery' of her poetry in 1845 would see the Brontë sisters enter print for the first time, much against Emily's wishes; Anne's journey to London in 1848 would bring tragedy back to the parsonage;[1] and in July 1835 Charlotte Brontë's commencement of her first job would also bring huge upheaval for Emily. Things would never be the same for the Brontë sisters.

Charlotte Brontë entered Roe Head School at Mirfield in January 1831, and remained there as a pupil until May 1832. It was a time of personal growth for Charlotte; not only did she greatly increase her knowledge on subjects such as history and geography, she also made close friends who would remain with her for the rest of her life.

Charlotte spoke of the school in glowing terms upon her return, especially of its headmistress and the kindly regime she ran. It was not expected, however, that Emily and Anne would follow Charlotte to school, but rather that she would impart the knowledge she had gained to her own sisters. Money was frequently tight at the parsonage, and although help from godparents and family friends had paid for Charlotte to attend school, Patrick could not impose on them to do the same for his remaining daughters.

Things changed in 1835, thanks to a wedding in the Wooler family. When Margaret Wooler opened her school in 1830, she did so with the assistance of four sisters who served as teachers. On 16 July 1835, Marianne Wooler married Reverend Thomas Allbutt, Vicar of Dewsbury,[2] a role formerly held by Patrick Brontë. As another sister had already married, Margaret was now left with half the number of teachers she once had to serve a growing number of pupils. A new teacher was urgently required, and thoughts turned to a young woman known to both Margaret and Marianne: Charlotte Brontë.

It is common knowledge how close Charlotte and Margaret Wooler became – the former headmistress did, after all, give Charlotte away at her wedding in 1854 – but it may also be that Marianne remembered her former pupil fondly, and that she kept in touch with the Brontës throughout their lives. A telling clue to this is contained within a 1925 obituary for Sir Thomas Clifford Allbutt. Sir Clifford (as he was known) was born in 1836 to Marianne and Reverend Allbutt, and he became an eminent scientist and a professor at Cambridge University. The obituary, however, focuses on another claim to fame, as it is headed 'A Link with the Brontës'. It reads:

> With the passing of Sir Thomas Clifford Allbutt, one of the last links with the Brontës was broken. He knew Charlotte Brontë when he was nineteen years of age, and also remembered seeing her sister Emily. This was by reason of the fact that he was the nephew of Miss Wooler, whose school at Roe Head was attended by the three Brontë sisters.[3]

It is safe to assume that this should read, 'he knew Charlotte Brontë when *she* was nineteen years of age', as this was the age at which she began teaching at the school, and the year in which the future Sir Clifford became 19 was the year that Charlotte died. Even so, this reading also makes little sense, as Emily had left Roe Head before he was born and Charlotte left while he was an infant. If we take the claims of this Cambridge don to be correct, it must mean that he, in the company of his mother or aunt, had met both Charlotte and Emily Brontë at a later date.

What we know for sure is that, after Marianne's wedding, Charlotte was given the opportunity to replace her at the school, and it was an offer she readily accepted. Charlotte had enjoyed teaching her younger sisters and being back in the bosom of her loving family, but she recognised that it was now her responsibility to make her own way in the world and by doing so ease the financial burden being placed upon her father. It was this that made the offer from Miss Wooler doubly attractive, for even though the salary itself was far from generous it also included an opportunity for her to take one of her sisters to the school to be taught free of charge; in this way, there would be two fewer mouths for Patrick to feed. As the eldest of her two sisters, Emily was the natural choice for this gift, and Charlotte wrote to Ellen Nussey to tell her of this development:

> Yes, I am going to teach in the very school where I myself was taught. Miss Wooler made me the offer, and I preferred it to one or two proposals of private governess-ship, which I had before received. I am sad – very sad – at the thought of leaving home; but duty – necessity – these are stern mistresses, who will not be disobeyed ... Emily and I leave home on the 29TH of this month; the idea of being together consoles us somewhat.[4]

As she embarked upon a new chapter of her life, one that would mark the end of her childhood years and the beginning of her adult responsibilities, Charlotte was convinced that Emily would enjoy being a pupil at Roe Head as much as she had, and that she herself would thrive as a teacher just as she had thrived as a pupil. On both of these assumptions she was very wrong.

Charlotte had completely misunderstood Emily's character. By now aged 17, she had already become fiercely independent and, as her diary paper of a year earlier had revealed, Emily liked to do her work when it suited her, not when she was told to do it. She loved to read and was an intelligent scholar who learned things quickly, but she wanted to be able to learn at her own pace, rather than being tied to a regimented schedule.

Emily soon found that learning at Roe Head School was very different to learning at Haworth Parsonage. It was dull and monotonous, with the main textbook employed being

Historical and Miscellaneous Questions for the Use of Young People by Richmal Mangnall.

Mangnall was born in 1769, and she attended the Crofton Hall School near Wakefield which was later graced by Maria and Elizabeth Brontë for a term. She died in 1820, but her fame and influence lived on for many decades, thanks to her tuition book of 1798 which became known as *Mangnall's Questions.* It was a book of questions and answers that covers a wide breadth of subjects, so that pupils could gain a comprehensive education simply through learning it by rote. It became a huge success, and was used in schools and by private tutors across the country – by the 1850s it had run to more than eighty editions. Unfortunately, this type of book-based learning was anathema to Emily Brontë, and she despised learning subjects that held no interest for her, just as she despised being deprived of in-depth learning on subjects that did interest her.

Doubtless Emily would have liked to pour out her heart on this matter to Charlotte, but Charlotte was also under a darkening cloud. The number of pupils had grown greatly from her own time as a scholar, when there were no more than ten pupils,[5] and she found herself much busier than she had anticipated. As the most junior teacher, she was also given charge of the youngest pupils, an age group that drove Charlotte to distraction and meant that she had little contact with her sister. Her personal despair at her situation was vented with spleen in a series of notes that became known as *The Roe Head Journal.* Charlotte leaves us in little doubt what she thought of her pupils and her job as a teacher:

> I had been toiling for nearly an hour with Miss Lister, Miss Marriott and Ellen Cook, striving to teach them the distinction between an article and a substantive ... The thought came over me: am I to spend all the best part of my life in this wretched bondage, forcibly suppressing my rage at the idleness, the

apathy and the hyperbolical and most asinine stupidity of those fat headed oafs, and on compulsion assuming an air of kindness, patience and assiduity?[6]

Emily had little opportunity to unburden herself to Charlotte, and she found her homesickness growing day by day: she missed walks on the wild moors that she loved so much, she missed the opportunity to talk about Gondal and dream up new plot lines, and she missed the person she did those things with – her sister Anne.

The regime at Roe Head was strict, yet kind, but it was completely unsuited to the young woman Emily had become. Used to simple fare, the varied diet was not to her taste and so she ate little; the pupils were not to her liking, and so she said little; and little by little she became very ill.

For Charlotte, the creeping illness overcoming Emily was terribly reminiscent of what had happened to Maria and Elizabeth when they were at school. She explained what happened in her 1850 biographical notice of Emily:

> She [Emily] found in the bleak solitude [of Haworth's moors] many and dear delights; and not the least and best loved – was liberty. Liberty was the breath of Emily's nostrils; without it, she perished. The change from her own home to a school, and from her own very noiseless, very secluded, but unrestricted and inartificial mode of life, to one of disciplined routine (though under the kindliest auspices) was what she failed in enduring. Her nature proved here too strong for her fortitude. Every morning when she woke, the vision of home and the moors rushed on her, and darkened and saddened the day that lay before her. Nobody knew what ailed her but me – I knew only too well. In this struggle her health was quickly broken; her white face, attenuated form, and failing strength threatened rapid decline. I felt in my heart she would die, if she did not go home.[7]

Charlotte wrote to her father begging him to call Emily home and, as he too had memories of Maria and Elizabeth imprinted on his mind, he readily agreed.

Emily's school adventure had ended and she returned to Haworth, where she made a rapid recovery. The embrace with which Anne greeted her was the best medicine she could get, but if she now envisaged months and years ahead composing Gondal tales with her sister she was mistaken. The offer at Roe Head still stood, and it was too valuable to resist. Anne Brontë was sent to take Emily's place at the school and, from a dated portrait of the school she created, we know that she was in place by October 1835. Emily's time at Roe Head, a stay that had made her so homesick it was feared she would die, had lasted less than three months.

At this point, it may have been expected that Emily would continue to complete her education at home in Haworth and settle down to a life of domesticity in the parsonage, but she was not so easily cowed and defeated. While her family would undoubtedly have been supportive, Emily was often her own harshest critic and would have been scornful of the weakness she had displayed. She still harboured a hope that she could make her own way in the world, and a letter from Charlotte to Ellen Nussey on 2 October 1838 reveals that Emily had put this plan into action: 'Emily is gone into a situation as teacher in a large school of near forty pupils near Halifax.'[8]

This must have been a shock announcement for Ellen, as there was no intimation of Emily's plans in any previous correspondence from Charlotte. The school she had entered was known as Law Hill, sometimes referred to as Cliff Hill, in Southowram, on the outskirts of Halifax. The school was run by a Miss Elizabeth Patchett, and Charlotte's letter intimates that Emily's move there was sudden. So, why did she make the 11-mile move from Haworth to Law Hill?

The factors that took Emily to Law Hill were exactly the same as those that had taken Charlotte to Roe Head as a teacher, two years earlier. Emily knew that she and her sisters would eventually have to make their own way in the world. Their father was now in his sixties and suffering from increasingly poor vision; if he was to become ill, or worse, they would be left destitute unless they had their own careers to call upon. She was also driven by a desire to prove to herself that she could survive away from the familiar scenery of home, and it was this combination that led to her sudden decision to accept an opportunity which mirrored the one Charlotte had accepted in 1835.

We have seen how Charlotte became a teacher after the marriage of a sister of the school's headmistress, and by coincidence the same sequence of events happened to Emily. On 21 September 1837, Maria Patchett married Titus Brooke at Southowram Church, presided over by Reverend John Hope.[9] Maria was a teacher at her sister Elizabeth's school, and so it was her marriage that led to the vacancy which Emily was employed to fill. The headmistresses Patchett, and Wooler of Roe Head, knew each other, and so it might have been Margaret Wooler's recommendation that secured Emily the job. If so, this recommendation can only have come via Charlotte's auspices rather than by any positive views on Emily's brief time as a pupil. It may also have helped that Charlotte had been school friends with Leah and Maria Brooke, sisters of the groom, Titus.

However Emily arrived at the Law Hill School, we know she was there just days after the wedding, and the early report we get from Charlotte is not a favourable one:

> I have had one letter from her [Emily] since her departure, it gives an appalling account of her duties – Hard labour from six in the morning until near eleven at night, with only one half-hour of exercise between – this is slavery, I fear she will never stand it.[10]

Emily's first impression of her new home would certainly have been a pleasing one, as it bore many resemblances to the one she had left behind at Haworth. Law Hill lies at the top of a steep climb rising up from Halifax itself. The pathway leading to it and the village of Southowram is even steeper than the famous incline of Haworth, and the views at the top were calculated to put a smile on Emily's face. Law Hill is surrounded on three sides by extensive moorland that rolls away from it, and the vista is as impressive today as it would have been to Emily in 1838.

The house is now in private hands, but it is still possible to see what a large and imposing building it is. The main house itself was where Miss Patchett lived and, as it is far too big for one person, it seems eminently likely that other teachers, including Emily, resided within it. Law Hill had previously been in the hands of the Walkers, a merchant family involved in the wool trade. A two-storey building formerly used as a warehouse was converted to school rooms, and the pupils slept in the upper-floor rooms.

The property had its own livestock kept in adjacent farm buildings and, as Miss Patchett was a keen horsewoman, there were stables too. Horse riding was part of the curriculum for the pupils at Law Hill, which gives an indication of the kind of establishment it was. Roe Head was a perfectly respectable school for the daughters of the wealthy new industrialist class, but Law Hill had a rather loftier reputation and was a boarding school for girls who came from upper- and upper middle-class backgrounds, rather than those tainted by association with new money.

The steep climb to Law Hill would have been second nature to Emily, and she would have appreciated both its moorland landscape and the proximity of animals, but the difficulties she had suffered at Roe Head began to resurface. The only report we have of Emily as a teacher comes from

Mrs Watkinson, who was interviewed sixty years later by the Brontë biographer Ellis Chadwick, and who was an 8-year-old pupil at the school at the time of Emily's service there. Based upon the memories of this pupil, Chadwick states that Emily made little impression on her charges. 'She had charge of the younger children, and they soon forgot the time she spent with them, though there is no record that she was ever unkind; on the contrary she was liked by some of her pupils.'[11]

It is another recollection of Mrs Watkinson, however, that is most telling: 'The one thing that impressed her most about Emily Brontë was her devotion to the house-dog, which she once told her little pupils was dearer to her than they were.'[12] This seems entirely in keeping with Emily's character, as there were few people whom she could feel a connection with as much as the dogs she loved, especially her famous pets, Grasper and Keeper. It is nevertheless a sign that Emily was finding the duties of a teacher (and especially the constant demands for attention from her pupils) trying, just as her more naturally gregarious sister Charlotte did.

Some commentators have felt that Charlotte's opinion of Emily's service at Law Hill is too harsh, and this was certainly the view of Miss Patchett herself, by then Mrs Hope, having married the vicar who had presided over her sister's wedding, when it appeared in Elizabeth Gaskell's biography of Charlotte. They point out that the school had an excellent reputation and that Miss Patchett had connections with some of the leading members of Halifax society, including Anne Lister of nearby Shibden Hall, who became famous in her own right for her frank diaries of the time. It is also reported that Miss Patchett often took her pupils to grand music concerts in Halifax and to the town's natural history museum, which had an impressive collection of stuffed birds.

These were all advantageous to the girls' education, but it does not necessarily mean that Emily got to enjoy the delights herself. Concerts and natural history museums were perfectly to Emily's taste, but if she only got to hear of them second-hand it would only have increased her despondency. We cannot hide from the fact that Charlotte's report to Ellen was based directly upon a letter that Emily had sent to Charlotte, and Emily, like her sister Anne, praised honesty above all other things.

It seems likely to me that Elizabeth Patchett kept things on a very tight rein at her school, which is precisely the reason that it became highly prized. Schedules would have been rigidly enforced, and lessons strictly planned and controlled. This was anathema to Emily Brontë. Her more haphazard way of working and living would have been completely out of step with what Miss Patchett wanted, and we can imagine this forthright woman letting Emily know that she would have to make rapid improvements in her conduct and performance.

Elizabeth Patchett was a formidable woman. She was still active, physically and mentally, well into her eighties, as a later occupier of Law Hill recalled:

> The present owner remembers the last visit paid by Mrs. Hope [Miss Patchett], the former schoolmistress. She was then a very old lady, but still beautiful with her grey curls, and, though over eighty years of age, 'could nip about from room to room quite gaily,' as he expressed it.[13]

Elizabeth was described as being very pretty, with her hair worn in curls even into old age, an excellent equestrian and well loved by her pupils. She could also be stern and forbidding, and her marriage to Reverend Hope, a Scotsman noted for his Presbyterian style of hellfire preaching, is an indicator of the severe, unbending beliefs that she held.

The temptation for Emily must have been to admit defeat at an early stage and yet, buoyed perhaps by the company of the house dog and the familiarity of the moors around her, she convinced herself that she could not go home again in an ignominious defeat. Emily struggled on, surrounded by people, but alone for the first time in her life. She survived two terms until the health-sapping home sickness once again became too much to bear. The nineteenth-century biographer Agnes Robinson explained:

> [Emily] came back to Haworth for a brief rest at Christmas, and again left for the hated life she led, drudging among strangers. But when spring came back, with its feverish weakness, with its beauty and memories, to that stern place of exile, she failed. Her health broke down, shattered by long-resisted homesickness. Weary and mortified at heart, Emily again went back to seek life and happiness on the wild moors of Haworth.[14]

Emily may have lasted little more than half a year in Halifax, but for a woman of her sensibilities this, in its own way, was a kind of triumph. She had faced the drear existence with courage, she had tried the life for which she was eminently unsuited. Most importantly for us, she had returned with two memories that would be put to great use later. Near to Anne Lister's Shibden Hall was the imposing High Sunderland Hall; now long disappeared, its physical appearance would be recreated in part as Wuthering Heights. As we shall see when we look at Emily's composition of this book, she would also draw heavily on an astonishing family feud that had taken place in Law Hill itself. The tumultuous and tormented months high on the hills above Halifax would, nine years later, lead to one of the greatest accomplishments in world literature.

9

THY MAGIC TONE

For him who struck thy foreign string,
I ween this heart hath ceased to care;
Then why dost thou such feelings bring,
To my sad spirit, old Guitar?
It is as if the warm sunlight,
In some deep glen should lingering stay,
When clouds of storm, or shades of night,
Had wrapped the parent orb away –
It is as if the glassy brook,
Should image still its willows fair,
Though years ago the woodman's stroke,
Laid low in dust their gleaming hair.
Even so, guitar, thy magic tone,
Hath moved the tear and waked the sigh;
Hath bid the ancient torrent flow,
Although its very source is dry!

('The Lady to Her Guitar', dated 30 August 1838)

MANY OF THE lessons that Emily taught at Law Hill School would have been totally unsuited to her skills and experience: for instance, she had to teach needlework despite being far from accomplished with a needle herself. The results were obviously far from satisfactory, as Ellis Chadwick concluded after talking to those who remembered Emily as a teacher:

> Her work was hard because she had not the faculty of doing it quickly. Unlike Charlotte, she was not good at needlework, and like her elder sister Maria, though clever in her own unique way, she was untidy and fond of day-dreaming.[1]

There was one subject Emily taught, however, in which she was more than proficient: music. We think of her today as a great novelist and poet, and rightly so, but she was a master of many artistic forms and was a skilled musician and accomplished painter.

In time, Emily became an excellent pianist, but as with all musicians, proficiency in the performance of music stems first from the enjoyment of listening to music. Opportunities for listening to music in the nineteenth century were, of course, far more limited than they are in our modern world where we take for granted the pleasure of listening to a beautiful song or tune. The only chance that Emily and her siblings would have had to experience music as children was through listening to live performances; but there were more of those available than you may think. The increasing industrialisation of northern England, and especially the introduction of the railways, brought an influx of labour to Yorkshire and Lancashire, much of it from Ireland. Some will have brought their favourite musical instruments with them in the form of penny whistles and fiddles, and Emily must have loved listening to them play the airs and jigs that came from the land of her forefathers.

There was also an increase in professional productions of music at this time, as well as shows put on by enthusiastic amateur musicians. One particularly grand concert in 1846 was staged in a location very well known to Emily: her father's church, a short walk from their parsonage. The concert at St Michael and All Angels Church was held on 20 July, just ten days before Emily's 28th birthday. An orchestra of eighty musicians took their place under the baton of Mr Whyte, and singers of note participated, including Mr Wilde from York and the local tenor, Thomas Parker. A local newspaper reported that the church was 'crowded to suffocation' and also noted the attendance of Reverend Brontë who, it said, was 'now totally blind'[2] (indeed, by this time Patrick's cataracts had left him almost unable to see).

Haworth is situated on a remote aspect of bleakly beautiful moorland, and life for many of its residents was tough and frequently short. Even so, it was a village that could appreciate the finer things in life and had a long history of loving and celebrating music. The Haworth Philharmonic Society was formed in 1780 and held concerts at regular intervals, including a spectacular annual concert that was held on 5 November in the Black Bull Inn adjacent to Reverend Brontë's church. The public house became all too well known to Branwell in his later years, but on the night of a concert it is likely that the Brontë family as a whole would have been in attendance.

These nights featured a diverse selection of music, and were happy events filled not only with the sweet sounds of arias but with the raucous sound of laughter as well, as this review of an 1834 concert at the Black Bull reveals:

The Philharmonic Society in this place [Haworth], held a concert in the Large Room of the Black Bull Inn, on Tuesday evening, April 1st. The songs, catches, and glees were well selected. Miss Parker sung with much sweetness, and was highly applauded. Mr. Parker was in fine voice, and sang with his usual effect. Mr. Clark sung several comic songs with much taste, and was often encored, particularly in the song of 'Miss Levi,' which kept the audience in continual laughter. The concert was very numerously and respectably attended, and the company went away highly gratified.[3]

A concert of a rather different kind had been held in Haworth just a week earlier and 23 March saw the official unveiling of a grand new organ at St Michael and All Angels Church. It was immediately put to good use with a concert performance of Handel's magnificent oratorio 'Messiah'. This was a moment of personal triumph for Patrick Brontë, who had been raising funds to purchase the instrument for a year. He used his noted powers of persuasion to cajole wealthy parishioners into making a donation, including one within his own home, as a letter to a parishioner on 17 September 1833 reveals:

> I have spoken to several people concerning the organ. All seem desirous of having one if the money can be procured. Miss Branwell says she will subscribe five pounds, and some others have promised to give liberally. Mr Sunderland, the Keighley organist, says he will give his services gratis on the day of the opening of the organ, and, in general, the real friends of the church are desirous of having one. A player can also be readily procured.[4]

Patrick Brontë took centre stage at the performance of 'Messiah', accompanied by his four children and sister-in-law, Elizabeth Branwell. Emily was dressed in her finest apparel and, seated alongside Anne, she was undoubtedly entranced by the fine music and singing, as we can see from copies of Handel's work in the sheet music books that she copied out in later years.

Music could move Emily to tears, as her poem 'The Lady to Her Guitar' shows, and she associated certain songs and airs with people and events in her life. It is evident that she found the sound of a guitar particularly moving, although we have no record of her ever having played one. The modern six-stringed guitar had originated less than thirty years before Emily's birth, commonly attributed to a Maestro Fabricatore of Naples, Italy.[5] It obviously did not take long for it to reach Haworth, and for its versatile sound to find a place in Emily's heart.

In this poem, the thought of the guitar's tone has produced a reflective, melancholy effect on the lady as she thinks back to earlier associations of the instrument with a person whose gleaming hair the woodman's stroke has long since laid low in dust. The poem being written in 1838, it is easy to conjecture that the guitar's music is calling to mind her sisters Maria and Elizabeth who had died thirteen years earlier.

Emily loved to listen to music, and this love naturally evolved into a desire to play music. She was joined by Anne in a petition to their father to help them in this desire, and he was happy to indulge them – particularly as the ability to play, and therefore teach, music would be helpful in any future career as a teacher or governess. In late 1833 or early 1834, Emily was delighted to find a new arrival in the parsonage – an upright cabinet piano.

Pianos were a sign of prestige and wealth throughout the nineteenth century, and a new piano would certainly have been beyond the means of Patrick. The model he bought was a second-hand one sold by John Green of Soho Square, London.[6] It was a basic model but, even so, it is likely that he received assistance in buying it from one or more of the children's godparents, and Aunt Branwell may have made a contribution to the purchase, as she was often wont to do.

Here was a purchase that all the family could enjoy. Branwell had already demonstrated his musical ability by becoming a proficient flautist, and he was now engaged in organ lessons from the Keighley organist, Abraham Stansfield Sunderland (Patrick obviously had his son in mind in his letter to parishioners when he spoke of being able to procure an organist). Sunderland's reward for the provision of lessons was to be gently mocked in an Angrian story, under the name of 'Mr Sudbury Figgs', who is called for when a 'fine and full new horgan was hoppened in Howard Church'.[7]

The piano allowed Branwell to practise his keyboard skills at home, but it soon became the firm favourite of Emily and Anne. Sunderland was now engaged to teach the two youngest Brontës as well, with supplementary lessons provided by local tutor, William Summerscale. The girls' natural talent for music was soon evident, leaving Branwell far behind. The lessons continued until late 1834,[8] by which time the girls had become proficient enough to teach themselves. A particular joy would perhaps have come when the girls shared the piano, Emily taking the keys on one half and Anne on the other. Alas, Charlotte was left a bystander as her eyesight was so poor that she found it difficult to read the score and was advised to refrain from playing for fear of straining her vision.

We get a first-hand report of the sisters' musical abilities from Ellen Nussey, and as a regular visitor to the parsonage she would have heard them playing often. 'Emily, after some application, played with precision and brilliancy. Anne played also, but she preferred soft harmonies and vocal music. She sang a little; her voice was weak, but very sweet in tone.'[9] When reading this praise, we should take into account that many middle-class families had pianos at this time, and consequently the general standard of playing was greater than it is today. In this light, Ellen's regard of Emily's playing is high praise indeed.

Ellen was not the only one to appreciate Emily's skills as a pianist; in Belgium, Professor Constantin Héger was so impressed with her ability that he arranged for a piano master from the Brussels Conservatory to hone her skills, after which she taught other pupils.

We know how enthusiastic both Emily and Anne were about music, and the type of music they liked, thanks to the large collection of their sheet music that is still in the Brontë Parsonage Museum, much of it copied out by their own hands. In fact, there are 111 music scores of Emily's, dating before the end of 1834 and showing the initial enthusiasm that filled them after the purchase of the piano, and in 1844 she purchased an eight-volume collection of 176 piano scores called *The Musical Library*.[10]

Among the scores were duets that Emily and Anne would have played together. We know that Anne favoured light and comic operas by the likes of Rossini and Mozart, but Emily's collection demonstrates an eclectic and sophisticated taste. We see works by Beethoven, Handel, Clementi, Dussek and Franz Liszt, whom Emily may have seen in person as he gave a concert in Brussels while she was there and also performed in Halifax in 1841. By comparing Emily's music scores of the mid-1830s and the mid-1840s, we see that she has pencilled in fingerings in the earlier scores, handwritten marks to show her which keys to play, whereas the later music is free of such markings, indicating that she was able to play the most complex music by sight by this time.

The fact that Patrick Brontë, despite the financial constraints under which he often operated, paid for music lessons for his daughters as well as his son showed his enlightened attitude compared to many fathers of the time. He believed that a comprehensive education was useful in its own right, and therefore as important for girls as it was for boys. This was demonstrated in the Sunday schools that he set up in both Thornton and Haworth, but also in the post-curricular tuition that he arranged for his daughters.

For much of their childhood, the Brontës' education was provided by Patrick and Aunt Branwell, but while they could, and did, teach them subjects such as history and geography, needlework, literature and Bible studies, they realised that some subjects lay outside of their skillset. Music was one such subject, and so was art. From an early age, all of the Brontë children had shown an enthusiasm for art, copying drawings from books as well as creating illustrations for many of their childhood stories. An example of this is the sketch of herself and her sister Anne at the table that Emily drew onto the corner of her 1837 diary paper.

Seeing the joy that it brought his children, and once again aware that it could be useful for their prospective future careers, Patrick arranged for all his children to be given art lessons by the accomplished artist and architect, John Bradley of Keighley.[11] Bradley taught the children during 1829 and 1830, and may have given extra lessons to the children in succeeding years, especially to Branwell, who attempted to establish a career for himself as a portrait artist. Bradley was an expert at capturing the buildings and landscapes around Keighley, focusing on the reality of everyday life rather than the grandeur that many painters would prefer, as shown in his series of pictures of 'Keighley Hovels'. By the time he taught Emily and her sisters, he had endured a series of personal tragedies, having watched four of his sons die within a year and half of each other.[12]

Bradley encouraged the children to learn by copying drawings in books such as Thomas Bewick's *The History of British Birds*. This book was a joy to all the children, but especially to the nature-loving Emily as it contained not only pictures of birds, exquisitely drawn by the author, but also rural scenes in general. They would later copy drawings from a series of books designed for artistic tuition. It was a good and solid basis for the children's artistic endeavours, and the early drawings of the Brontës showed excellent promise.

Emily was never one to be satisfied at copying the works of other people, however, or to concentrate on the still life pictures that were then considered most fitting for women to draw, so she soon developed a style of her own. It is unfortunate that we do not have more of Emily's artwork, because what has survived is vibrant and exciting. It is fitting that much of Emily's extant artwork is of the Brontë pets. Thus, we see an 1834 black and white portrait of her dog Grasper, which captures the spirit of the animal so completely that we can imagine it leaping off the page and into Emily's arms. In contrast to this, we have Emily's picture of Anne's spaniel Flossy; it is a joyous portrait of the dog chasing a bird across the moors. Bewick's influence, and therefore the influence of the art teacher John Bradley, can be most seen in Emily's portrait of her pet merlin, Nero. Perched on a tree branch with one leg in the air, the hawk is given an almost human air of sophistication, and the green foliage in the background helps to lift the picture above the black and white illustrations favoured by Thomas Bewick.

It is obvious that Emily Brontë was an accomplished artist, just as she was a brilliant pianist, and these became activities that she enjoyed throughout her life, acting as a release from the stresses and mundanity of everyday life in the parsonage. Emily's music would also have been called upon to entertain, or to raise the spirits of others. Patrick, in the days when he lived in perpetual darkness, loved to sit and listen to Emily play the piano while Anne sang sweetly along. After the death of his two daughters within six months of each other in 1848 and 1849, Patrick had the piano removed and hidden away in an upstairs room. Just the sight of the piano that had brought so much joy to him now evoked memories of the kind and brilliant daughter who had played it. Like the guitar of Emily's poem, the sheer physical presence of the piano was enough to move the tear and wake the sigh. It was more than he could bear.

10

I SEE HEAVEN'S GLORIES SHINE

No coward soul is mine,
No trembler in the world's storm-troubled sphere,
I see Heaven's glories shine,
And Faith shines equal arming me from Fear,
O God within my breast,
Almighty ever-present Deity,
Life, that in me hast rest,
As I Undying Life, have power in Thee,
Vain are the thousand creeds,
That move men's hearts, unutterably vain,
Worthless as withered weeds,
Or idlest froth amid the boundless main,
To waken doubt in one,
Holding so fast by thy infinity,
So surely anchored on,
The steadfast rock of Immortality.
With wide-embracing love,
Thy spirit animates eternal years,
Pervades and broods above,

Changes, sustains, dissolves, creates and rears,
Though earth and moon were gone,
And suns and universes ceased to be,
And Thou wert left alone,
Every Existence would exist in thee,
There is not room for Death,
Nor atom that his might could render void,
Since thou art Being and Breath,
And what thou art may never be destroyed.

('No Coward Soul is Mine', dated 2 January 1846)

'N o Coward Soul is Mine' is probably Emily Brontë's most famous poem, and one of the most celebrated poems of the nineteenth century. Its opening line can even be found adorning t-shirts, an expression of strength, resilience and individuality. Emily had all these qualities and more, but the wearers of said t-shirts may not be aware just how radical her poem was, as it was the proclamation of a belief that would have seen her shunned by polite society. It is a poem about religion and faith, and in this, as in many other ways, Emily walked her own path.

By the time Emily wrote this poem, her father Patrick had been a minister in the Church of England for more than forty years, but during that period the Anglican Church had changed greatly, and divisions were becoming ever more apparent between traditional and evangelical factions. The increased fragmentation of the Church, and the increasing popularity of Methodism and Baptism in the north of England, also brought societal tension, which frequently threatened to spill over into violence.

Calvinism was becoming increasingly powerful within the official Church. Founded by the Frenchman John Calvin in the sixteenth century, it was distinguished for its strict beliefs, and its insistence upon the fatality of sin and the division between the elect and the damned. Taken to its extreme, this meant that some people were destined to go to hell once they had committed even the most minor of misdemeanours, while others, known as the elect, could commit any sin that they wished with impunity as they were already chosen for heaven. Unsurprisingly, most Calvinist preachers saw themselves as the elect.

This inflexible belief system was ridiculed in the brilliant and bitingly satirical gothic horror novel *The Private Memoirs and Confessions of a Justified Sinner* by James Hogg. Hogg was known as 'the Ettrick Shepherd', a reference to his lowly Scottish origins, and he was a regular contributor to *Blackwood's Magazine* so loved by the Brontës. It seems certain that Emily Brontë had read *The Private Memoirs and Confessions of a Justified Sinner*, as it is one of the books whose influence can clearly be felt in *Wuthering Heights*.

For an archetypal example of a Calvinist priest at this time, we can look at Reverend William Carus Wilson. His sermons were long, and unrelenting in their depictions of hellfire and damnation. He was against worldliness of any kind, as it was sure to lead to infernal torments – even for a minister of the Church, as this extract from one of his sermons shows:

> The worldliness even of the most moral and (in the general acceptance of the term) respectable Clergyman, oh! How it eats as a canker at the roots of his pastoral usefulness, and discourages many a young disciple who was beginning to turn his face Zionwards.[1]

Carus Wilson wrote this particular sermon about the failings of modern ministers and the decline in piety of the clergy to mark the visit to his church by the Bishop of Chester, so we can see that he was not a man to mince his words. He believed that he was setting a store of treasures for himself after his death, but in fact his memory is now widely criticised and ridiculed, thanks to a former pupil of his. It was Wilson who founded the Clergy Daughters' School at Cowan Bridge where Maria and Elizabeth Brontë died. Charlotte would never forget or forgive his role in this, and depicted him as the cruel and heartless Mr Brocklehurst in *Jane Eyre*.

In a memorable scene, we see Brocklehurst berating the young Jane and telling her that she is forever doomed as a sinner:

> 'Do you know where the wicked go after death?'
>   'They go to hell,' was my ready and orthodox answer.
>   'And what is hell? Can you tell me that?'

> 'A pit full of fire.'
>
> 'And should you like to fall into that pit, and to be burning there for ever?'
>
> 'No, sir.'
>
> 'What must you do to avoid it?'
>
> I deliberated a moment; my answer, when it did come, was objectionable: 'I must keep in good health, and not die.'[2]

Moderates in the Church of England were under threat, not only from Calvinism but also from the emergence of evangelical sects such as the Baptists and the Methodists. The Methodist movement was founded by the brothers Charles and John Wesley in the early decades of the eighteenth century. Initially it remained part of the official Church, but later it split from the Anglican communion. There were significant differences of opinion within the Methodist Church too – with a harder line that became known as Calvinistic Methodism being represented by the likes of George Whitefield and William Grimshaw.

Grimshaw was one of the most famous Methodist ministers of the eighteenth century, a charismatic preacher who could draw huge crowds to his sermons: and for the last twenty-one years of his life he was minister at St Michael and All Angels Church in Haworth. He was renowned for his zealous, passionate sermons, and also for their inordinate length. He was also a rigid enforcer of attendance at church on Sunday, and had a rather uncompromising way of enforcing it:

> He sometimes gave out a very long Psalm (tradition says the 119TH) and while it was being sung, he left the reading-desk, and taking a horsewhip went into the public-houses, and flogged the loiterers into church. They were swift who could escape the lash of the parson by sneaking out the back way.[3]

Perhaps surprisingly, this no-nonsense approach proved highly popular, and Grimshaw sometimes held services on the open moors outside Haworth to crowds of thousands who had come from across the north of England. Grimshaw's reputation endured into the nineteenth century, so that Patrick Brontë knew his appointment to the curacy of Haworth was a prestigious and historically important one.

One member of the parsonage, in particular, held the memory of Reverend Grimshaw in high esteem: Aunt Branwell had a commemorative William Grimshaw teapot, which bears on one side the phrase, 'To me, to live is Christ, to die is Gain', and on the reverse, 'Wm Grimshaw, Haworth'. Methodism was even stronger in Cornwall than it was in Yorkshire, and the Branwell family of Penzance were staunch supporters of the faith. Nevertheless, Aunt Branwell dutifully attended the Church of England services presided over by her brother-in-law, although many of her fellow Methodists did not.

The problem for Patrick, and for the Church of England in general in the early decades of the nineteenth century, is that although Grimshaw had been an Anglican minister, his followers now had churches of their own to attend, and they became much more popular than St Michael and All Angels. An ecclesiastical survey was taken on Sunday 30 May 1851. It showed that 383 people had attended the three services at Patrick's church. However, 422 had attended Lower Town Wesleyan Methodist Church, 424 had attended West Lane Baptist Church, and 900 had attended Hall Green Baptist Church.[4]

The survey revealed that just 15 per cent of church-goers in Haworth went to the official Church of England services, and yet every adult had to pay a tithe, known as a church rate, to St Michael and All Angels, whether they attended it or not. This, understandably, was a source of great discontent among the villagers, known as Dissenters, who attended non-official services, and only Patrick's forceful nature and general good standing within the village allowed him to collect the tax without provoking an uprising. Even so, for three years there was a stand-off between Patrick and the villagers, during which no church rates at all were collected. After a meeting at Hall Green Baptist Church on 27 February 1837, a delegation proposed that they send a petition to parliament asking for the complete abolition of church rates. A local newspaper reported Patrick's furious response:

> The church parson and his curate have been in a dreadful state of excitement ever since. On last Sabbath morning one of them commenced a fierce attack upon all Dissenters; and in the afternoon both of those meek-spirited clergymen let loose a whole volley of vulgar abuse, in a double lecture in the church, to the great consternation of the congregation.[5]

If Patrick Brontë could, on occasion, launch stern words against the Dissenters of his parish, he showed much more tolerance with his own children, for in fact all four of his children who lived into adulthood had difficulties with the teachings of the Church.

Anne Brontë was, without doubt, the Brontë child with the strongest faith, and yet it was her deep questioning of religious matters that led to a physical and mental breakdown in December 1837. She was then a pupil at Roe Head School, but Calvinist teachings troubled her so much that her thoughts were haunted by ideas of hell for herself and those she loved. This led to a complete collapse, until a Dissenting minister, James la Trobe, was brought to talk to her on what could have been her deathbed. Later made a bishop in the Moravian Church, he recalled the event thus:

> She was suffering from a severe attack of gastric fever which brought her very low, and her voice was barely a whisper; her life hung on a slender thread. She soon got over the shyness natural on seeing a perfect stranger. The words of love, from Jesus,

opened her ear to my words, and she was very grateful for my visits. I found her well acquainted with the main truths of the Bible respecting our salvation, but seeing them more through the law than the gospel, more as a requirement from God than His gift in His Son, but her heart opened to the sweet views of salvation, pardon, and peace in the blood of Christ, and she accepted His welcome to the weary and heavy laden sinner, conscious more of her not loving her Lord her God than of acts of enmity to him, had she died then, I would have counted her His redeemed and ransomed child. It was not until I read Charlotte Brontë's 'Life' that I recognised my interesting patient at Roe Head.[6]

Anne now developed her own idea of God that was at odds with the official teaching of the day – a God who was loving, forgiving and offered redemption for everybody, whatever their sins. This sustained her throughout her life, although she still suffered agonising doubts from time to time.

After the lessons from Abraham Sunderland, Branwell duly became organist at his father's church, but his faith fell away until he stopped attending church altogether. Only on the day of his demise did he finally respond to prayers being said over him with a heartfelt 'amen'.

Even Charlotte harboured some religious doubts and fears, specifically regarding the reality, or otherwise, of heaven and the everlasting spirit. We get an indication of this in *Jane Eyre* when the young Jane visits Helen Burns, modelled on her sister Maria, on the night before her death:

'But where are you going to, Helen? Can you see? Do you know?'

'I believe; I have faith; I am going to God.'

'Where is God? What is God?'

'My Maker and yours, who will never destroy what he created' …

'You are sure then, Helen, that there is such a place as heaven, and that our souls can get to it when we die?'

'I am sure there is a future state; I believe God is good; I can resign my immortal part to Him without any misgiving ... You will come to that same region of happiness; be received by the same mighty, universal Parent, no doubt, dear Jane.'

Again I questioned, but this time only in thought. 'Where is that region? Does it exist?'[7]

This is a question that all the Brontë children must have asked when alone with their own thoughts, or possibly in whispered candlelit conversations. It was certainly a question that vexed Emily Brontë, but as her poem at the head of this chapter reveals, she came up with a very different answer to that of her siblings.

Emily's faith was deeply personal and, like much in her life, deeply private. Those closest to her would have been aware of her increasing isolation from the views of the official Church: bound strictly by the word of the Bible, and with a set of moral instructions that had to be followed at all times, they were never likely to find favour in the independent-minded Emily. As she grew older, she still joined the family procession to the church, but it was evident from her demeanour that while she was there in person she was far from there in spirit. An observer of her in the church at this time could not forget her behaviour:

Emily made a lasting impression. One who saw her many times told of 'the stolid stoical manner of Emily as she sat bolt upright in the corner of the pew, as motionless as a statue. Her compressed mouth and drooping eyelids, and indeed her whole demeanour, appeared to indicate strong innate power.'[8]

Eventually, like her brother, Emily stopped attending church services, but her family knew better than to ask her the reason why, as we can see from her brief yet to the point response to a question asked to Mary Taylor. Mary was a great friend of Charlotte, and a remarkable woman in her own right. She left her home in Gomersal in the West Riding of England and emigrated to New Zealand, where she set up a successful business. She later returned to England and became a feminist writer. Her family were frequenters of the Moravian Church, a Dissenting sect popular in Yorkshire that had originated in what is now the Czech Republic. Somebody asked Mary Taylor to explain her views on religion, and we may guess that it was Charlotte and that she had asked a similar question of Emily. The forthright Mary responded that 'religious opinions were between the individual and God', to which Emily tersely responded, 'That's right.'[9]

Emily kept silent about her beliefs, but the truth about the nature of her faith surfaces time and again in both her poetry and her prose. It is not correct to say that Emily is atheist or agnostic, as her brother Branwell probably was, because her poetry often refers to a god, as in 'No Coward Soul is Mine', for example, but it is clear that this is not the Christian God that her father spoke of in his sermons. This god does not exist in heaven, an all-powerful deity, who rules us all from afar, but rather he lives within Emily herself as an almighty and ever-present spirit.

The solitary excursions on the moors that Emily took while her sisters were in the wooden pews of church were not an escape from religion, they *were* her religion. Emily believed that an all-powerful spirit was in every living thing, in the birds in the sky and the bluebells on the ground, as much as in herself. It was a self-realised form of nature worship akin to modern forms of paganism, and she left us plentiful evidence of what it meant to her. It was a faith built upon the power of nature, but with a deity ruling over it. To Emily, there were spirits everywhere which were invisible to most people but not always to her.

There are other examples of such visionaries in the world of literature. William Blake springs to mind, as does Samuel

Taylor Coleridge, who woke to find that he had composed a vast epic poem called *Kubla Khan* in a dream but was famously interrupted during his transcription of this poem by a 'visitor from Porlock'. After the man had gone, recollection of the poem disappeared too, leaving us with only fifty-four wonderful lines beginning, 'In Xanadu did Kubla Khan,/ A stately pleasure-dome decree'.

Coleridge's visions were drug induced, of course, but Emily needed little more than candlelight in a darkened room for the visitor that she often calls to in her poems. We have already seen an example of this in her poem 'To Imagination', when she talks of the phantom bliss of the benignant power that comes her in the quiet of the evening, but it is a recurring theme in much of Emily's best verse.

Emily is not the only Brontë to write of visions that come to her when she is in a creative mood. A young Charlotte, in her Roe Head journal, wrote:

> The toil of the day, succeeded by this moment of divine leisure, had acted on me like opium & was coiling about me a disturbed but fascinating spell, such as I never felt before. What I imagined grew morbidly vivid. I remember I quite seemed to see, with my bodily eyes, a lady standing in the hall of a gentleman's house, as if waiting for some one.[10]

This vision confused and disturbed Charlotte, but similar and even more powerful visions were welcomed with open arms by Emily. It is worth noting Charlotte's assertion that she saw the vision with her bodily eyes rather than it being part of a dream. This is clearly the case with Emily's visions too, and it calls to mind what modern practitioners of the occult call 'astral projection'. They believe that through a practice of meditation, concentration and willpower the spirit can leave the human body and travel at will to astral planes where other spirits exist, and where they can then interact with them.

Whether this actually happens, or is a trick of the mind, I leave you to decide, but what is quite clear is that these people believe it is happening, and that their perception of their visions is as real as the things they see in everyday life.

Emily's visions were not only of rooms and vague impressions of people, but of a recurring spirit that was central to her creative process. It had a human form and talked to Emily, and through the development of this theme in Emily's work we can see that while, at first, she dreaded its presence she soon came to love its visitations. The first recording we have of this vision comes in a remarkable poem dated November 1837. In it, Emily writes as if the vision addresses her and she also reveals the physical symptoms, the strange sensations that grip her before her visions appear:

> I'll come when thou art saddest,
> Laid alone in the darkened room ...
> I'll come when the heart's real feeling,
> Has entire unbiased sway,
> And my influence o'er thee stealing,
> Grief deepening joy congealing,
> Shall bear thy soul away.
> Listen 'tis just the hour,
> The awful time for thee,
> Dost thou not feel upon thy soul,
> A flood of strange sensations roll,
> Forerunners of a sterner power,
> Heralds of me.[11]

By February 1844, the visions have become a regular and welcome visitor, as we see from the title of Emily's poem 'My Comforter' and its closing lines:

> No: what sweet thing resembles thee,
> My thoughtful comforter?

And yet a little longer speak,
Calm this resentful mood;
And while the savage heart grows meek,
For other tokens do not seek,
But let the tears upon my cheek,
Evince my gratitude.[12]

Even at times when she felt herself in peril, this spirit ensured that she could not be broken. This much is clear in her poem *The Prisoner*, which also contains the revelation that Emily knew her visitations were not something experienced by most people, but a blessing unique to her and others like her. The poem is set in Gondal, with its protagonist in a dungeon, a common theme in many Gondalian poems, but it is a metaphor for the times Emily felt herself trapped or downtrodden:

A messenger of hope, comes every night to me,
And offers for short life, eternal liberty,
He comes with western winds, with evening's wandering airs,
With that clear dusk of heaven that brings the thickest stars.
Winds take a pensive tone, and stars a tender fire,
And visions rise, and change, that kill me with desire.[13]

The visionary spirit came to her typically in the dark of night, when she was alone in her tiny room overlooking the barren parsonage garden and the crowded graveyard beyond. It would come when Emily's moods were at their most extreme, whether in sorrow or joy, and its presence would leave Emily elated. But what exactly was it? To Emily, the answer was clear – the spirit came from within her, and was an integral part of her own being. This is at the heart of Emily's faith; it can be seen in 'No Coward Soul is Mine' when she talks of the god within her breast, and is also central to 'The Philosopher', perhaps the most explicit of all Emily's visionary poems about her beliefs and the most vibrant in its depiction of her visions, as we can see in the following lines:

Three gods, within this little frame,
Are warring night and day;
Heaven could not hold them all, and yet,
They are all held in me;
And must be mine till I forget my present entity! ...
I saw a spirit, standing, man,
Where thou doth stand – an hour ago,
And round his feet three rivers ran,
Of equal depth, and equal flow –
A golden stream – and one like blood;
And one like sapphire seemed to be;
But, where they joined their triple flood,
It tumbled in an inky sea.[14]

It is perhaps telling that when the 'three gods' within Emily meet, represented by the gold, red and blue streams of her vision, they tumble in an inky sea: in other words, when the spirits come together it is then that she has the greatest creative ability and can put her words down in ink.

The poem talks of a trinity of gods, but it is far removed from the Christian Holy Trinity preached by her father. Emily was harking back to an earlier pagan trinity, a belief that is as old as humanity itself, with the triple aspects of nature, such as the waxing moon, full moon and waning moon, representing the natural cycle of birth, life and death.

There is also, in 'The Philosopher', a reference to something else that had become a core belief of Emily's variety of paganism: the eternal spirit. As a child, Emily heard her father and aunt preach about the importance of striving for eternal life in heaven, but as she grew older this image of a cloud-based paradise seemed very different to her own ideals. In the moorland environment, barren and brutal in winter yet teeming with life in summer, she saw the endless natural cycle of death and rebirth, and it was this and the visions that she experienced which led to a belief in reincarnation.

In 'The Philosopher', she talks not of death, but of the moment when 'she forgets her present entity'. It is a belief that she returns to in another Gondal poem 'Lines by Claudia', when she writes:

In English fields my limbs were laid,
With English turf beneath my head,
My spirit wandered o'er that shore,
Where nought but it may wander more.
Yet if the soul can thus return,
I need not and I will not mourn,
And vainly did you drive me far,
With leagues of ocean stretched between,
My mortal flesh you might debar,
But not the eternal fire within.[15]

Emily was using the cover of Gondal to talk about beliefs that were close to her own heart, yet which would have been seen as shocking if revealed by her own voice rather than behind the fictional mask of Claudia. Emily's most famous expression of what happens to the soul after death, namely that it is reborn upon Earth rather than being confined to heaven, is found not in her poetry but in her brilliant prose. Just as Emily believed her soul was immortal, although the form carrying it would change, so Catherine has become an immortal character in literature, taking on new meanings for new generations of readers:

Heaven did not seem to be my home; and I broke my heart with weeping to come back to earth; and the angels were so angry that they flung me out into the middle of the heath on the top of Wuthering Heights; where I woke sobbing for joy.[16]

Emily Brontë's belief system in the supremacy of nature, a god that existed within each living thing, a spirit world that could be seen in visions, and reincarnation, would have been scandalous to most in the first half of the nineteenth century. Nevertheless, these beliefs became central to Emily's life and to her writing, and are one reason that the world of Gondal, of creativity, became as real to her as the world her siblings lived in. Once she had discovered her own personal truth there could be no abandoning it – after all, hers was no coward soul.

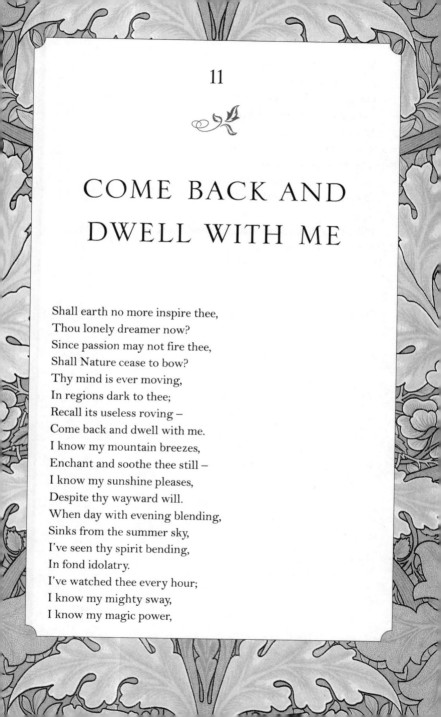

COME BACK AND DWELL WITH ME

Shall earth no more inspire thee,
Thou lonely dreamer now?
Since passion may not fire thee,
Shall Nature cease to bow?
Thy mind is ever moving,
In regions dark to thee;
Recall its useless roving –
Come back and dwell with me.
I know my mountain breezes,
Enchant and soothe thee still –
I know my sunshine pleases,
Despite thy wayward will.
When day with evening blending,
Sinks from the summer sky,
I've seen thy spirit bending,
In fond idolatry.
I've watched thee every hour;
I know my mighty sway,
I know my magic power,

To drive thy griefs away.
Few hearts to mortals given,
On earth so wildly pine;
Yet none would ask a heaven,
More like this earth than thine.
Then let my winds caress thee –
Thy comrade let me be –
Since nought beside can bless thee,
Return and dwell with me.

('Shall Earth No More Inspire Thee', dated 16 May 1841)

THE MIGHTY POWER that Emily writes of in this poem is clearly another reference to the visionary spirit that often aided her compositions, but she held a similar magic power over someone very close to her: her sister Charlotte. When she needed inspiration or respite from doubts or depression, it was inevitably Emily who could lift her spirits and drive her grief away.

Charlotte Brontë paid a moving tribute to her sisters Emily and Anne after their early deaths, in which she emphasised how different they were to the perceptions of those who saw or knew them briefly. 'I may sum up all by saying, that for strangers they were nothing, for superficial observers less than nothing; but for those who had known them all their lives in intimacy of close relationship, they were genuinely good and truly great.'[1]

Charlotte was a deep-thinking and complex woman, which is one reason why her writing sparkles as it does. She could be a severe critic, as shown by her pronouncements on her pupils at Roe Head and her judgement on writers such as Jane Austen. Writing to a critic, she asks, 'Why do you like Miss Austen so very much? I am puzzled on that point ... I should hardly like to live with her ladies and gentlemen in their elegant but confined houses.'[2] Once she had made a friend, however, she was a friend for life and fiercely loyal. Although her friendships with Ellen Nussey and Mary Taylor were stronger than any that her sisters made, her closest bond of all was with Emily.

In some ways, it may seem strange that they should grow so close, as they were very different characters. Even though Charlotte was shy, she was far more capable of mixing in society than Emily, and while Charlotte liked to have her forceful say on any and all matters, Emily would often remain tight-lipped. We also have the difference in religious temperament and beliefs covered in the previous chapter to consider, but Emily's insistence upon keeping her unorthodox beliefs to herself ensured that this did not drive a wedge between her and Charlotte, or between her and the devoutly Christian Anne.

One thing Charlotte loved more than anything else was strength, and she realised from an early age that beneath Emily's quiet front was a strong interior, and a spirit that was unlike any other she had witnessed. In their childhood years it was Emily's physical strength that was apparent: she was by far the tallest of the Brontë children, including Branwell, and despite her wiry frame she was the strongest too, in later years physically carrying her brother up the parsonage staircase when he was too drunk to walk up himself.

Emily's creative power was also apparent to Charlotte from the first, and we shall see in Chapter 15 how her astonishment at the power of Emily's verse provoked a rare, yet passionate, argument between the two, and also provided the catalyst that led to the Brontë books we so love today.

Charlotte's role as the eldest sister after the deaths of Maria and Elizabeth in 1825 saw her become almost a mother figure at times to her younger siblings, and yet her admiration for Emily soon developed into a hero worship, second only to that of her love for the Duke of Wellington. Emily was all the things Charlotte longed to be: she was tall while Charlotte was unusually short, she was a natural poet whereas Charlotte's verse was often formulaic and overly long, she was lithe and graceful and Charlotte was often clumsy, and she was practical and could easily master domestic duties, whereas Charlotte managed to burn the clothing on her first attempt at ironing. In later years, Charlotte would be oblivious to Emily's increasing eccentricities which left her almost confined to her house and the moors around it, seeing it as just another example of her strength and independent nature. Charlotte would always strive to make a living, would always do what people expected of her, but Emily would only do things on her terms. How Charlotte wished that she could be just like her.

Charlotte also saw, as did all who knew her intimately, another side of Emily's character – one that is often overlooked today. While Emily was typically quiet with strangers, she could be very different with friends, and she also had a wicked sense of humour. Charlotte was often the brunt of her tricks, as Ellen Nussey recalled:

A spell of mischief also lurked in her [Emily] on occasions. When out on the moors she enjoyed leading Charlotte where she would not dare to go of her own free will. C. had a mortal dread of unknown animals and it was Emily's pleasure to lead her into close vicinity and then to tell her of what she had done, laughing at her horror with great amusement.[3]

All who came to know Emily realised that, although she could be quiet and sphinx-like, she was very kind at heart. They also knew that Emily could be very stubborn, and once she had made her mind up she was unlikely ever to change it, even if it was to the detriment of herself. We hear this near the end of Emily's life, in a plaintive letter that Charlotte sent to her friend and publisher, W.S. Williams:

It is best usually to leave her to form her own judgement and especially not to advocate the side you wish her to favour; if you do she is sure to lean in the opposite direction, and ten to one will argue herself into non-compliance.[4]

It was this lifelong stubbornness, and her ability to make others do what she wanted, that in happier and healthier times had led William Weightman to bestow a nickname upon Emily that stuck: 'the Major'. The fact that it was a playful nickname and not one that Emily objected to was shown by the fact that even Anne used it, closing an 1847 letter to Ellen Nussey with the words, 'Accept my best love and I must not omit the Major's compliments.'[5]

Emily had the aloof bearing, but also the innate strength, of a nineteenth-century army officer, but Charlotte herself took comfort and strength from this. It was for this reason, in addition to the usual filial regard, that Charlotte enjoyed being in Emily's company so much. She may have sat or stood silently, but her nearby presence was in itself comforting, and as Charlotte grew older and encountered the challenges that adult life could bring, she needed this comforting familiarity more and more.

It is interesting to note the contrast between Charlotte's relationship with Emily at Roe Head School, and her relationship with Anne at the same establishment. She is oblivious to her youngest sister's sufferings until it is almost too late, a realisation that would fill Charlotte with guilt for the rest of her life. This is partly because of the teaching duties that Charlotte was completely unsuited to, and partly due to the lack of contact between the two sisters during the school day. This far from satisfactory state of affairs, as far as the sisters were concerned, was also present when Emily was a pupil, but on that occasion Charlotte watched her sibling with an eagle eye, so sensitive to her sister's thoughts and disposition that she begged her father to remove Emily from the school even before a physical illness had taken hold.

As Charlotte grew older, she turned increasingly to Emily for support and as a person to look up to, in what was a change in the Brontë family dynamics. After the deaths of Maria and Elizabeth the four remaining siblings, although undoubtedly a loving and close unit as a whole, separated into two factions: Charlotte and Branwell, and Emily and Anne. The most obvious sign of this is the little books written exclusively by Charlotte and Branwell, whereas Emily and Anne would have to wait for Charlotte to enter school before they would begin their own joint literary venture. There would sometimes be a physical distance of miles between Emily and Anne, but there would never be any lasting division between them. The same could not be said of Charlotte and her brother.

In her childhood she, like the rest of the Brontës, had looked upon Branwell as the great hope of the family. He had often been a mischievous child, yes, but he had shown talent and kindness too, and Charlotte hoped he would become a breadwinner for the family if ill health, or worse, should end their father's labours. By the time she had taken up her own post as a teacher in 1835, it had become clear that Branwell as an adult would find it hard to live up to his childhood promise, and disillusionment set in. The close ties that had bound Charlotte and her brother as children became increasingly frayed as the years passed, until they were severed altogether by Branwell's descent into a drink- and drug-fuelled inferno. By then Charlotte had ceased speaking to him altogether, substituting Emily in his place as the family member to turn to in a crisis.

She found Emily steadfast, reliable and predictable: rock-like foundations that her admiration was built upon. While it may be said that there were tensions between Charlotte and Anne from time to time, with the elder sister being jealous of Anne's looks, her seeming closeness with William Weightman and the success of her second novel *The Tenant of Wildfell Hall*, the green-eyed monster would never come between Charlotte and Emily.

The primacy of the elder sister in Charlotte's opinion became particularly obvious at the beginning of 1842, when two out of the three Brontë sisters embarked upon an overseas adventure. Charlotte had decided to attend a school in Brussels to learn languages, reasoning this would help the Brontës attract pupils to a school that they intended to set up. We will look into this, and in particular the effect it had upon Emily, in Chapter 13, but for now we will consider why Charlotte chose Emily, rather than Anne, to go with her.

On the face of it, Anne would have seemed the more obvious choice to accompany her sister to Brussels. On the downside, she was in a valued position as governess to the Robinson family, near York, at the time, although it was a position that Anne would have been only too happy to leave. She had also proved that she could exist in a world outside of Haworth

Parsonage, which was more than Emily had done. Emily, by contrast, had lasted just a matter of weeks in her only other experience as a pupil, and she was also proving invaluable within the parsonage at the time by carrying out many of the domestic duties.

Despite this, Charlotte was in no doubt that it was Emily who should travel with her to Belgium, a clear indication of the supremacy of Emily over Anne in Charlotte's mind. During their time together in Brussels, Charlotte must have felt vindicated in her decision: there was no mental collapse as there had been at Roe Head, and being together did indeed console them somewhat, just as Charlotte had hoped it would six and a half years earlier when they made the shorter journey to school at Mirfield.[6]

Another indication of the growing esteem in which Charlotte held Emily, and the value she gained from having this sensible and reliable sister around, can be seen in the difference in Charlotte's experience in Brussels before and after Emily left. Emily arrived back in Haworth in November 1842, happy to resume her domestic duties in the parsonage that she loved so much. Charlotte, in particular, had thrived during their months together in the Belgian capital, but after returning alone in January 1843 Charlotte found the following year a terrible ordeal.

In her second spell at Brussels' Pensionnat Héger, Charlotte acted primarily as a teacher rather than pupil and, just as at Roe Head, she found it a position that was completely unsuitable to her fiery and restless temperament. The need to provide constant attention to the scholars, rather than being alone with her thoughts as she wished, wore her down. What made things worse, in Charlotte's opinion, was that the pupils were predominantly Catholic, a faith that she, like many English people at the time, had very little time for. Her disdain for what she saw as popish idolatry is obvious in her two Brussels-based novels, *The Professor* and *Villette*, as the following extract demonstrates:

Sylvie was gentle in manners, intelligent in mind. She was even sincere, as far as her religion would permit her to be so ... her whole soul was warped to a conventual bias, and in the tame, trained subjection of her manner one read that she had already prepared herself for the future course of her life by giving up her independence of thought and action into the hands of some despotic confessor ... She was the model pupil of Mlle Reuter's establishment – pale, blighted image, where life lingered feebly, but whence the soul had been conjured by Romish wizard-craft.[7]

Given this unflinching attitude, what Charlotte did on 1 September 1843 seems remarkable, but it is testimony to her troubled mind, being alone without the sister she adored. She walked into the Catholic Cathedral of St Gudula, which was close to the Pensionnat Héger. She not only remained in the church, but sought out a priest and asked to make a confession. This was completely at odds with her own beliefs, and she knew it would appear scandalous to most who knew her, but she also knew there was one person she could turn to who would not judge her. She wrote to Emily the following day, unburdening herself in writing as she had so often done face to face:

An odd whim came into my head. In a solitary part of the Cathedral six or seven people still remained kneeling by the confessionals. In two confessionals I saw a priest. I felt as if I did not care what I did, provided it was not absolutely wrong, and that it served to vary my life and yield a moment's interest. I took a fancy to change myself into a Catholic and go and make a real confession to see what it was like. Knowing me as you do, you will think this odd, but when people are by themselves they have singular fancies ... I actually did confess – a real confession ... I think you had better not tell Papa of this. He will not understand that it was only a freak, and will perhaps think I am going to turn Catholic.[8]

By sending this letter, Charlotte had transformed Emily into another confessor. She too was put under an oath not to reveal the confession to anyone, and it was, of course, a command that Emily kept. Just what was it that Charlotte needed to confess to? At our distance of time and with Charlotte's novels and letters as evidence, the answer is obvious – she had fallen in love with her married professor, Constantin Héger.

Héger was the prototype of the strong and stern heroes of Charlotte's novels, and she undoubtedly found his strict demeanour captivating. With Emily by her side in 1842, she had managed to keep her emotions under control but, as she says in the letter above, when she was by herself she developed singular fancies. It is the absence of Emily, then, that allows Charlotte to spiral out of control in Brussels. As the familiar, dark despondency settled upon her, she knew there was only one answer – she had to go back to her comrade, to the one who truly inspired her; she would go back and live with Emily again.

Charlotte returned to Haworth in 1844 in low spirits, feeling heartbroken and defeated. Over the course of a year, she continued to write to M. Héger, but the letters became increasingly desperate as he failed to reply. 'To forbid me to write to you, to refuse to reply to me – that will be to tear from me the only joy I have on earth, to deprive me of my last remaining privilege – a privilege I will never renounce voluntarily.'[9] The letter was cut into pieces by M. Héger.

This was a time of trial and torment for Charlotte, but Emily was at hand to guide her through it, dependable as always; it was a time that would strengthen their relationship still further. Emily was providing the strength and common-sense advice that Charlotte most needed, and it is these qualities that are most evident in Charlotte's portrayal of Shirley Keeldar. Charlotte told Elizabeth Gaskell that her eponymous heroine was based upon Emily, but it was a depiction of how she could be in different circumstances:

The character of Shirley herself, is Charlotte's representation of Emily ... we must remember how little we are acquainted with her, compared to that sister who, out of her more intimate knowledge, says that she 'was genuinely good, and truly great,' and who tried to depict in Shirley Keeldar, as what Emily Brontë would have been, had she been placed in health and prosperity.[10]

Shirley sees Charlotte looking beyond the straitened circumstances of her sister's life, and instead depicting the immense potential that she believed Emily had. It is a noble portrait, and one that reveals the intense love Charlotte had for the sister born two years after her. While we see images of Shirley, by which we of course mean Emily, as a rich heiress, we also see moments that are a photographic image of the sister that Charlotte knew and so admired:

In Shirley's nature prevailed at times an easy indolence. There were periods when she took delight in perfect vacancy of hand and eye-movements when her thoughts, her simple existence, the fact of the world being around and heaven above her, seemed to yield her such fullness of happiness that she did not need to lift a finger to increase the joy. Often, after an active morning, she would spend a sunny afternoon in lying stirless on the turf, at the foot of some tree of friendly umbrage ... No spectacle did she ask but that of the deep blue sky, and such cloudlets as sailed afar and aloft across its span; no sound but that of the bee's hum, the leaf's whisper.[11]

In *Shirley* we see how Charlotte feels Emily would have been if she had been given a position of power in life, and the money to support it. She is stronger than any man, facing down an armed insurrection at one point. It was how Emily could be, but more than that, to Charlotte it was how Emily actually was. This much was made clear in Charlotte's moving tribute to her sister in her 1850 *Biographical Notice of Ellis and Acton Bell*. Charlotte knew, as did all who came to know her, that Emily's death had left the world diminished; she was as unique as she was great:

Day by day, when I saw with what a front she met suffering, I looked on her with an anguish of wonder and love. I have seen nothing like it; but, indeed, I have never seen her parallel in anything. Stronger than a man, simpler than a child, her nature stood alone.[12]

SECRET PLEASURE,
SECRET TEARS

I am the only being whose doom,
No tongue would ask, no eye would mourn;
I never caused a thought of gloom,
A smile of joy, since I was born.
In secret pleasure – secret tears,
This changeful life has slipped away,
As friendless after eighteen years,
As lone as on my natal day.
There have been times I cannot hide,
There have been times when this was drear,
When my sad soul forgot its pride,
And longed for one to love me here.
But those were in the early glow,
Of feelings since subdued by care;
And they have died so long ago,
I hardly now believe they were.
First melted off the hope of youth,
Then Fancy's rainbow fast withdrew;
And then experience told me truth,

In mortal bosoms never grew.
'Twas grief enough to think mankind,
All hollow, servile, insincere –
But worse to trust to my own mind,
And find the same corruption there.

('I am the Only Being Whose Doom', dated 17 May 1839)

I T WAS OFTEN difficult to discern Emily's moods and feelings from one moment to the other, so adept was she at keeping them feelings hidden even from those who were closest to her. This was another thing that she had in common with Anne, of whom Charlotte wrote (in relation to some scathing reviews that had come in for *The Tenant of Wildfell Hall*), 'She does not say much for she is of a remarkably taciturn, still, thoughtful nature, reserved even with her nearest of kin, but I cannot avoid seeing that her spirits are depressed sometimes.'[1]

There is one major difference between the temperaments of the two youngest Brontës, however. Anne overcame this shyness when she had to, stirring herself into action and forcing herself to confront the outside world. As Emily got older she chose a different path, retreating into the safety of the parsonage and shunning the outside world and those who inhabited it. Haworth Parsonage had become Emily's prison, but it was an act of self-incarceration.

An excellent prison guard, Emily kept her emotions under lock and key, but when she did reward someone with a smile it was a moment that lingered long in the memory, as Ellen Nussey recalled:

Her extreme reserve seemed impenetrable, yet she was intensely loveable. She invited confidence in her moral power. Few people have the gift of looking and smiling, as she could look and smile – one of her rare expressive looks was something to remember through life, there was such a depth of soul and feeling, and yet shyness of revealing herself, a strength of self-containment seen in no other. She was in the strictest sense a law unto herself, and a heroine in keeping to her law.[2]

Charlotte, too, had noticed the power of Emily's smile, a smile that often came after a moment of silent meditation, as she revealed in her portrait of her sister as Shirley Keeldar:

Her sole book in such hours was the dim chronicle of memory or the sibyl page of anticipation. From her young eyes fell on each volume a glorious light to read by; round her lips at moments played a smile which revealed glimpses of the tale or prophecy. It was not sad, not dark.[3]

As a child, Emily's cheerful nature had charmed the teachers at the Clergy Daughters' School as well as the Heatons of Ponden Hall, and we have seen from the accounts above how a smile from her in adulthood could still prove irresistible. Yet, as she progressed through her teenage years and into adulthood, these smiles, moments of emotional frankness, became much less freely bestowed.

Emily wrote 'I am the Only Being Whose Doom' when she was 20 years old, despite the reference within it to being friendless after eighteen years, and it is a clear indication of the despondency that could fall upon her, hidden from others. Just what is it that had transformed the smiling child into a young woman who felt that she was incapable of bringing a moment's joy into the life of anyone?

To find the answer we must first head back to Cowan Bridge. At this point, the infant Emily was happy and gregarious, but although her tender years may have offered her some protection, she would still have felt the loss of Maria and Elizabeth. Did she somehow blame herself for the loss of her sisters, her young mind being incapable of understanding the true nature of disease and death?

By 1839, the year of the composition of the poem, Emily had also failed as a scholar at Roe Head, unable to last even a handful of months at a benign school with an enlightened learning environment. Her father and aunt welcomed her back to their parsonage with open arms, happy that she had escaped the fate which had threatened to engulf her as it had engulfed Maria and Elizabeth years earlier. But Emily was a sterner judge on herself – as the last lines of her poem reveal, the worst thing of all was to look into her own mind and find within the same weakness and corruption that she scorned in others.

Even more pertinently, this bleak poem of self-recrimination comes just two months after Emily had left her post at Miss Patchett's school at Law Hill. Emily had convinced herself that she was now made of sterner stuff than she had been at Roe Head, and while it is true that she had endured longer before returning to Haworth, she had suffered the same overpowering anxieties, loneliness and home sickness. Youthful hope had now melted away, as Emily came to the realisation that she could not function in the external world as other people could. With this reality ever at the forefront of her mind, she retreated further into herself, and into the familiar surrounds of Haworth Parsonage.

Solace would come from the moments she enjoyed with her sisters and brother, particularly those spent on the moors with Anne or walking around and around the dining table at evening time, composing tales and poems of Gondal. When she retired to her room, however, and watched the candle flickering before her eyes, the torment and self-doubt returned: was her life burning away like the wax before her?

There were nights, as we have seen, when Emily would find comfort in the visions that drove her creativity, but although these would leave her elated when they happened, they brought with them despair when they ended, as Emily reveals in her poem beginning 'How long will you remain? The midnight hour':

I'm happy now and would you tear away,
My blissful dream that never comes with day?
A vision dear though false for well my mind,
Knows what a bitter waking waits behind.[4]

There is another reason for Emily's low spirits evinced in her poem of May 1839, as it was composed two months after her beloved sister Anne had left Haworth to take up a position as governess to the Ingham family of Mirfield. The village she associated with her failure at Roe Head School had now taken the company she desired most away from her, and she had no way of knowing when Anne would return to her side. Anne's stay in Mirfield was a brief one, and she was back in Haworth at the end of the year, but by May 1840 she had accepted a new post with the Robinsons of Thorp Green Hall, a position that she held for more than five years.

While Anne made brief returns to the parsonage over Christmas, it was a six-year period during which Emily became increasingly isolated and introverted. With Charlotte often away too, and Branwell's behaviour becoming ever more erratic, she turned for company to a succession of pets. Emily's love of wildlife has become almost legendary, worshipping the hardy species that thrived on the moors, but she also loved the domestic animals that were present throughout her life. There was the hawk, Nero, and a canary named Dickie, as well as a pair of geese named after the royal princesses, Adelaide and Victoria. There were also cats, a black cat named Tom and a tortoiseshell cat called Tiger, and of course Emily's famous dogs, Grasper and Keeper.

Keeper was a huge mastiff, the size of which can be gauged by looking at his broad brass collar on display at the Brontë Parsonage Museum. He was also fierce, and it was said that only Emily could control him. Elizabeth Gaskell reported the gruesome tale of how Emily tamed Keeper by beating him into submission one night, after which event the dog became besotted with its mistress and would never leave her side.[5] While it seems that Emily did have to use force to tame Keeper on this occasion, it may well be that Gaskell has exaggerated the lengths to which she went. What is undoubted is that the dog and its owner loved each other dearly, as reported by Ellen Nussey, and as also evinced by Keeper's loyalty to his mistress even after her death, as we shall see in the final chapter of this book.

Such was Keeper's bond with Emily that he was reproduced in *Shirley* as the title character's four-legged companion, Tartar: fierce and yet fiercely loyal, it was a picture drawn by Charlotte from real life. There is also an incident in *Shirley* based upon an event in Emily's life that could have had devastating consequences for her. Shirley Keeldar sees a dog running past, panting and looking as if it has been ill used. She intends to bring the dog indoors to give it food and water but the dog bites her arm and runs off. Shirley is then informed that the dog is raging mad. Fearful of rabies, she takes immediate action:

'I walked straight into the laundry, where they are ironing most of the week, now that I have so many guests in the house. While the maid was busy crimping or starching, I took an Italian iron from the fire, and applied the light scarlet glowing tip to my arm. I bored it well in. It cauterized the little wound. Then I went upstairs.'

'I dare say you never once groaned?'

'I am sure I don't know. I was very miserable – not firm or tranquil at all, I think. There was no calm in my mind ... I was sitting at the foot of the bed, wishing Phoebe had not bitten me.'

'And alone. You like solitude.'

'Pardon me.'

'You disdain sympathy.'[6]

In these last three lines, Charlotte had accurately summed up her sister's attitude to suffering: if it could not be mastered then it had to be endured in silence and alone. The extract from Shirley seems almost fantastical, but in fact it is an almost exact description of what had happened to Emily in real life when she tried to comfort an unknown dog, as Charlotte once admitted to Elizabeth Gaskell.[7]

With the comforting presence of her siblings often absent, Emily did find happiness of a sort with the animals that she loved. She also eventually attained the self-respect she often lacked by throwing herself into the domestic side of life in the parsonage; and discovering that she excelled at it.

For most of Emily's life, Tabby Aykroyd served as chief housekeeper at the parsonage, but she was already in her mid-fifties by the time she arrived there. In the winter of 1836 she slipped on ice on the treacherous Main Street of Haworth, breaking her leg. It never fully healed, and it seemed likely that Tabby would have to leave her employment, but she was held in high regard by the Brontë children and, after their heartfelt pleas, she was kept on. Even so, the children had to take over some of the household tasks, and this became even more of a necessity when an infection in Tabby's leg in November 1839 necessitated her removal to her sister Susanna Wood's house to recuperate. She returned to the parsonage in 1842, but her role now was simply to provide some familiar company to Emily, who had taken over the role of housekeeper: it was a role Emily relished.

A letter from Charlotte to Ellen Nussey on 21 December 1839 reveals how this new arrangement was going:

> I manage the ironing and keep the rooms clean – Emily does the baking and attends to the kitchen. We are such odd animals that we prefer this mode of contrivance to having a new face among us. Besides we do not despair of Tabby's return and she shall not be supplanted by a stranger in her absence. I excited Aunt's wrath very much by burning the clothes the first time I attempted to iron but I do better now.[8]

It was not long before Emily took over ironing duties too.

We heard earlier, from family friend John Greenwood, how Emily's bread was deemed to be the best in the village, and this was a vital and laborious task at a time when all the daily bread for the parsonage was made by hand. To save time, she managed to combine the preparation of dough with her daily lessons, which she still kept up, as we can see from Mrs Gaskell's account based upon the conversations she had with Haworth villagers:

> It was Emily who made bread for all the family; and any one passing by the kitchen-door, might have seen her studying German out of an open book, propped up before her, as she kneaded the dough; but no study, however interesting, interfered with the goodness of the bread, which was always light and excellent.[9]

It may seem strange that a woman so filled with the creative spirit and so independently minded as Emily should gain a sense of fulfilment from domestic duties that would typically be carried out by a servant. She found that these tasks, from the baking of bread to the sweeping of flagstones, helped to relieve the tedium of the non-creative daylight hours and, even more importantly, they allowed her to be of practical use to her family. After her brief adventures at Roe Head and Law Hill, Emily had convinced herself that she would never be able to make a financial contribution to her family's upkeep, and this had a deleterious effect upon her moods and her self-worth. Now, however, she was carrying out a vital role, and in doing so she was sparing her father the expense of paying someone else to do it. It is perhaps no surprise that most of Emily's great poems, and her great novel, came when she was also acting as baker and housekeeper, as it was these tasks that were finally bringing her contentment rather than the doubt and loathing expressed in 'I am the Only Being Whose Doom'.

Emily's efforts not only gave her a sense of satisfaction, they were appreciated by her sisters too, with Anne writing, 'Emily ... is as busy as any of us, and in reality earns her food and raiment as much as we do',[10] and Charlotte providing similar praise: 'Emily is the only one left at home, where her usefulness and willingness make her indispensable.'[11]

The house that Emily kept so well is similar yet different to the parsonage that we can visit today. An extra wing was added to the house by Patrick's successor, Reverend John Wade. Outbuildings present in the nineteenth century, including the two-seater privy, are no longer there, and the internal dimensions of the rooms have also been altered. Charlotte made modifications to the house after the deaths of her sisters, so that Emily's room, as it is today, is narrower than it would have been when she slept and wrote there. One thing that has not changed is the narrow window from Emily's room which looks down onto the garden below and the graveyard adjoining it. (Gardening was perhaps the only domestic skill that Emily failed to master. She did make an attempt at it, encouraged by Ellen, but it was unsuited to the temperament of a woman who preferred the natural environment at its wildest.)[12]

Taking on the role of housekeeper allowed Emily to be where she most wanted to be, at Haworth Parsonage, but it also increased her estrangement from the world beyond it. Emily was well liked by the villagers, some of whom probably felt sorry for the parson's daughter who was surely destined to become an old maid, but she had very little interaction with them. She even excused herself from Sunday school teaching duties, something that Charlotte, Anne and Branwell undertook with varying degrees of success, although this may also have been due to her own lack of belief in the lessons the children were given.

As the 1840s progressed, Emily Brontë became an increasingly introverted woman, one whose mood could change from one day to the next. There are, unfortunately, few letters from Emily known to exist today, but two that she sent to Ellen Nussey show the peaks and troughs of her moods. In the first cheery missive, dating from 1845, she writes to tell Ellen that Charlotte can remain with her in Hathersage (where Ellen's brother was vicar and which would be recreated as Norton in *Jane Eyre*) for another week:

Dear Miss Ellen, if you have set your heart on Charlotte staying another week she has our united consent; I for one will take everything easy on Sunday – I'm glad she's enjoying herself: let her make the most of the next seven days & return stout and hearty.[13]

Two years earlier, she had sent Ellen a letter with a gloomier tone and revealing that even the act of writing a letter was too much for her at that moment:

All here are in good health, so was Anne according to the last accounts – the holidays will be here in a week or two and then if she be willing I will get her to write you a proper letter, a feat that I have never performed.[14]

Emily Brontë as an adult woman was one who had both secret pleasures and secret tears, but her outward appearance would remain enigmatically the same. She saw the life stretching before her as one of domestic duty in Haworth Parsonage for as long as she could see, but she could not have known that events would soon take her first away from her home and her country, and then onto an unsought literary stardom.

13

ANOTHER CLIME, ANOTHER SKY

A little while, a little while,
The noisy crowd are barred away;
And I can sing and I can smile,
A little while I've holiday!
Where wilt thou go my harassed heart?
Full many a land invites thee now;
And places near, and far apart,
Have rest for thee, my weary brow –
There is a spot 'mid barren hills,
Where winter howls and driving rain;
But, if the dreary tempest chills,
There is a light that warms again.
The house is old, the trees are bare,
And moonless bends the misty dome;
But what on earth is half so dear –
So longed for as the hearth of home?
The mute bird sitting on the stone,
The dank moss dripping from the wall,
The garden-walk with weeds o'ergrown,

I love them – how I love them all!
Shall I go there? or shall I seek,
Another clime, another sky,
Where tongues familiar music speak,
In accents dear to memory?
Yes, as I mused, the naked room,
The flickering firelight died away;
And from the midst of cheerless gloom,
I passed to bright, unclouded day –
A little and a lone green lane,
That opened on a common wide;
A distant, dreamy, dim blue chain,
Of mountains circling every side –
A heaven so clear, an earth so calm,
So sweet, so soft, so hushed an air;
And, deepening still the dream-like charm,
Wild moor-sheep feeding everywhere –
That was the scene – I knew it well;
I knew the pathways far and near,
That winding o'er each billowy swell,
Marked out the tracks of wandering deer.
Could I have lingered but an hour,
It well had paid a week of toil;
But truth has banished fancy's power:
I hear my dungeon bars recoil –
Even as I stood with raptured eye,
Absorbed in bliss so deep and dear,
My hour of rest had fleeted by,
And given me back to weary care.

('A Little While, A Little While', dated 4 December 1838)

EMILY BRONTË'S POEM of 1838, written while she was at Law Hill School high above Halifax, reveals her longing for the old house at Haworth. It is a love poem to the parsonage, and a sign of the all-consuming homesickness that brought to an end her only attempt at gainful employment just a few months later. The writer of that poem would surely have been amazed if she could have looked ahead another three years and find herself living, not just 11 miles away from Haworth but over 400 miles away in a completely different country.

While Emily was, more or less, contented with her new role as parsonage housekeeper, Charlotte had bigger plans for herself and her sisters. By December 1841 she had, after nine months, left a position as governess to the White family of Upperwood House at Rawdon, between Bradford and Leeds. Once again, she had found the act of teaching children too much of a strain to bear, but she had reached the conclusion that teaching itself was not the problem, rather the locations and circumstances that she had encountered. If she had her own school she could choose whom she taught, how she taught and where she taught them.

With the roles of governess or teacher always seeming their most likely future, the Brontë sisters had from an early age talked of running their own school, working together and reaping the rewards. It was a youthful dream, but in the summer of 1841 Charlotte, Emily and Anne began to discuss the matter more seriously, and had started to seek the financial backing they knew they would need. As the eldest sister, it is perhaps hardly surprising that Charlotte took the lead in the organising of the matter, but Anne also was enthusiastic about the idea, as she was beginning to tire of her role as governess to the Robinsons. Emily was less enamoured at the prospect of re-entering teaching, but she recognised its potential as a way to secure the financial future of the three girls, and it would also ensure they were not separated again.

Emily's enthusiasm for the scheme at this time can be seen from her discussion of it in her diary paper, written on 30 July 1841:

A scheme is at present in agitation for setting us up in a school of our own. As yet nothing is determined but I hope and trust it may go on and prosper and answer our highest expectations. This day 4-years I wonder whether we shall still be dragging on in our present condition or established to our heart's content. Time will show – I guess that at the time appointed for the opening of this paper, we i.e. Charlotte, Anne and I – shall be all merrily seated in our own sitting-room in some pleasant and flourishing seminary having just gathered in for the midsummer holidays. Papa, Aunt and Branwell will either have been, or be coming, to visit us – it will be a fine warm summery evening, very different from this bleak look-out. Anne and I will perchance slip out into the garden a few minutes to peruse our papers. I hope either this or something better will be the case.[1]

This is a rather touching account, full of youthful enthusiasm. Emily and Anne had, by now, developed the routine of writing a diary paper that would be opened by the other sister in four years' time. It is particularly revealing of Emily's main attraction to Charlotte's school scheme; she would be close to Anne again, and they would be able to spend beautiful summer evenings writing about Gondal together.

Anne also mentions the plan in her corresponding diary paper, but striking a rather more pessimistic tone: 'We are thinking of setting up a school of our own but nothing definite is settled about it yet and we do not know whether we shall be able to or not – I hope we shall.'[2] Anne is displaying her characteristic common sense, but perhaps she already had misgivings about her role in the school and felt that Charlotte was planning to freeze her out. Before the end of the year, the plans had changed dramatically and they would see her remaining at Thorp Green Hall while her sisters were treading foreign soil.

At the time Emily and Anne wrote their diary paper, a seemingly ideal situation presented itself. Margaret Wooler, whose school was now situated at Dewsbury Moor rather than Roe Head, planned to retire and, in a letter, she offered Charlotte the building at a very reasonable rent. With this in mind, Charlotte, then at Rawdon, wrote to her aunt for funds that would allow them to realise their dream of having their own school. Thanks to her relatively wealthy background, Aunt Branwell had considerably greater funds than their father, and despite her stern reputation she had shown that she could be generous, and that she wanted her nieces to get on in life. As revealed in a letter to Ellen, Charlotte was pleasantly surprised at her aunt's positive response:

> I have often you know said how much I wished such a thing [starting a school] but I never could conceive where the capital would come from for making such a speculation – I was well aware indeed, that Aunt had money – but I always considered that she was the last person who would offer a loan for the purpose in question. A loan however she has offered or rather intimates that she perhaps will offer in case pupils can be secured.[3]

Before serious negotiations could be entered into with Miss Wooler and Aunt Branwell, however, a letter from an old school friend had changed Charlotte's mind completely. Mary Taylor had left the West Riding of Yorkshire for Brussels, joining her younger sister Martha at the exclusive Château de Koekelberg finishing school. Mary wrote to Charlotte declaring the beauty of Brussels, its architecture and its museums. As Charlotte admitted in a letter to Ellen, Mary's missive left her with 'such a strong wish for wings'[4] that she despaired at the thought that she would not get to see the city herself. It was but a short moment from despair, however, until hope rose again as Charlotte discerned a way for her to join her friends in Belgium. Once again, she would need her aunt's financial assistance, and her letter to Aunt Branwell is a masterpiece of tact:

My friends recommend me, if I desire to secure permanent success, to delay commencing the school for six months longer, and by all means to contrive, by hook or by crook, to spend the intervening time in some school on the continent ... I would not go to France or Paris, I would go to Brussels in Belgium ... In half a year, I could acquire a thorough familiarity with French. I could improve greatly in Italian, and even get a dash of German ... These are advantages which would turn to vast account, when we actually commenced a school – and, if Emily could share them with me, only for a single half-year, we could take a footing in the world afterwards which we could never do now. I say Emily instead of Anne; for Anne might take her turn at some future period, if our school answered ... Papa will perhaps think it a wild and ambitious scheme; but who ever rose in the world without ambition? When he left Ireland to go to Cambridge he was as ambitious as I am now. I want us <u>all</u> to go on. I know we have talents, and I want them to be turned to account. I look to you, aunt, to help us. I think you will not refuse.[5]

Charlotte was anticipating the anxiety of her father, and producing the argument to counter it, as well as negating any suspicion Aunt Branwell may have that her favourite niece Anne was unfairly being left out of the plan. Charlotte's tact prevailed, and in time her aunt did supply the money to pay for the schooling of herself and Emily in Belgium. Charlotte would also, however, have to defend herself against the latter charge from another source: Emily.

Emily had reconciled herself to the idea of becoming a teacher as long as her sisters were by her side, and as long as they were within visiting distance of the rest of the family, but this was a different proposition altogether. Charlotte now wanted her to leave England behind and commit to spending half a year, and a considerable sum of their aunt's money, in Brussels. If her crushing homesickness resurfaced, she would not be able to return to Haworth as easily as she had from Mirfield and Halifax, and she had one particularly pressing concern: Anne's absence from their Belgian adventure.

We do not have a letter sent by Emily to Charlotte at Rawdon, but we do have Charlotte's reply, so we can be sure that Emily had been championing the sister whom she loved (while at the same time probably hoping Anne would take her place so she could remain in Haworth). Charlotte's response left Emily in little doubt, however, that it was imperative that she, rather than Anne, accompany her sister:

Anne seems omitted in the present plan, but if all goes right, I trust she will derive her full share of benefit from it in the end. I exhort you all to hope. I believe in my heart this is acting for the best; my only fear is lest others should doubt and be dismayed. Before our half-year in Brussels is completed you and I will have to seek employment abroad.[6]

Here was a terrifying new twist for Emily; not only would she be committed to Belgium for half a year, as she originally believed, but Charlotte now expected them to remain in the country for an indefinite period after that, meaning she would in all likelihood have to return to teaching. From the days of excitement Emily revealed in her July diary paper, she now plunged into fear and despair, but this time she refused to surrender to these negative emotions. Wrestling with the twin serpents in her mind, she at last conquered them. Emily agreed to join Charlotte, not only because she felt it would allow them to return to England and open a school, and certainly not because she revelled in the prospect of learning new languages and ideas, but because she wanted to prove to herself that she was not a hopeless cause: that she was stronger in spirit than she had once been.

It was the sternest test she faced in her life to that date, and she triumphed. Those who did not know her could scarce have guessed the courage and determination Emily needed to board the train bound for London, and then on to the ship that was sailing for Belgium. But Charlotte knew, and she later paid tribute to her sister's determination and fortitude:

> She went with me to the continent. The same suffering and conflict ensued … Once more she seemed sinking, but this time she rallied through the mere force of resolution; with inward remorse and shame she looked back on her former failure, and resolved to conquer in this second ordeal. She did conquer; but the victory cost her dear. She was never happy till she carried her hard-won knowledge back to the remote English village.[7]

After a short journey by gig from Haworth to Leeds, Emily joined her sister Charlotte on the train to Euston on the morning of Tuesday, 8 February 1842. Accompanying them on the journey was Mary Taylor and her brother Joe, whose business often took him to Brussels, and one other member of the party: Patrick Brontë. Charlotte's appeal to Patrick's ambition when he left Ireland for Cambridge not only met with his approval, it fired his enthusiasm.

Recalling happy memories of his journey from Ireland to England, he joined his daughters on their journey, saw them safely into their new school, and then spent some days on his own in Belgium and France before returning to Haworth. One of the sites he visited was the battlefield of Waterloo, just 10 miles south of Brussels, a site that fascinated Patrick, who hero-worshipped the Duke of Wellington just as much as did his daughter Charlotte.

Patrick had taken his preparation seriously, copying some handy French phrases into a handsewn book that is today part of the Brontë Parsonage Museum collection, and he also assisted with his daughters' preparation. Even with their aunt's financial backing, the Koekelberg school frequented by the Taylors was beyond the means of the Brontës. Knowing this, Patrick contacted an old acquaintance, Reverend Evan Jenkins, who was now the Anglican chaplain, not only to the British Embassy in Brussels but also to King Leopold I of Belgium. Jenkins, after some research into the matter by his wife, had no hesitation in recommending the Pensionnat Héger: it was reasonably priced, and yet well respected and eminently respectable, and it was there that Emily and Charlotte arrived on 15 February 1842.

Waiting to greet the women, now aged 23 and 25 respectively, was the owner of the establishment, and of the boys' school next door, Mme Claire Héger. A courteous and yet formal woman, she was then 38 years old and heavily pregnant with her fourth child. Three other teachers lived within the pensionnat, with a further seven tutors visiting from time to time to teach specific subjects. Among these was one who taught primarily at the boy's lycée, Mme Héger's husband, Constantin.

The school itself was a grand building in an equally grand location on the Rue d'Isabelle, sitting betwixt the upper town with its Place Royale and the lower town, still adorned with medieval houses, known as the Basse-Ville. In *The Professor*, Charlotte provides a description of the scene that met her and Emily as they first made their way to the school:

> I saw what a fine street was the Rue Royale, and, walking leisurely along its broad pavement, I continued to survey its stately hotels, till the palisades, the gates, the trees of the park appearing in sight offered to my eye a new attraction. I remember, before entering the park, I stood a while to

contemplate the statue of General Belliard, and then I advance
to the top of the great staircase just beyond, and I looked down
into a narrow back street, which I afterwards learned was
called the Rue d'Isabelle. I well recollect that my eyes rested
on the green door of a rather large house opposite, where, on a
brass plate, was inscribed, 'Pensionnat de Demoiselles' ... some
of the demoiselles, externats no doubt, were at that moment
issuing from the door. I looked for a pretty face amongst them,
but their close little French bonnets hid their features. In a
moment they were gone.[8]

This is an accurate description of the locale of the school that
Emily and her sister attended, situated at the foot of a grand
series of steps leading to a statue of General Belliard. Belliard
was a French Ambassador who had been instrumental in the
fight for Belgian independence. Belgium had only existed as
a country for twelve years when the Brontës arrived, and the
city of Brussels was full of memories of its violent split from
the Netherlands. It was also still full of soldiers and their
families from the Battle of Waterloo seventeen years earlier. It
is estimated that the English community in Brussels numbered
around 2,000 at this time, most of them having a connection
to the Waterloo battlefield.[9]

Charlotte found this English presence comforting amidst
the strange Catholic surroundings in which she found
herself, but it did little to ease Emily's alienation: whether
the people she met were from England or Belgium, she had
little in common with them and had no desire to make their
acquaintance. One solace for Emily was the continual company
of Charlotte, in marked contrast to her time at Roe Head when
her sister's teaching duties had kept them apart.

The pensionnat was housed in a large building, with the
upper floor based around a long dormitory in which all the
girls slept. In deference to their older age compared to the
other pupils and their upbringing as daughters of a clergyman,

Mme Héger had allocated the Brontës beds at the far extremity of the dormitory, with a curtain around to give them privacy. It was a kind gesture, and did much to help Emily overcome the homesickness which still haunted her, but when daylight came she still had to face the terror that was other people.

Two months after she arrived at the pensionnat, another family of English girls began lessons there – the Wheelwright sisters, Julia, Sarah, Frances, Emily and Laetitia, aged between 7 and 14. Emily remained aloof from them, but Charlotte later became firm friends with the eldest girl, known as Tish. Many years after their time at the school, the biographer Clement Shorter asked them for their memories of Emily's time as a fellow pupil, and they were less than complimentary. Laetitia responded:

> I am afraid my recollections of Emily Brontë will not aid you much. I simply disliked her from the first; her tallish ungainly ill-dressed figure contrasting so strongly with Charlotte's small, neat, trim, person, although their dresses were alike; always answering our jokes with 'I wish to be as God made me' … Charlotte was so devotedly attached to her, and thought so highly of her talents.[10]

This is a report that reflects worse upon the Wheelwrights than it does upon Emily. This group of five young girls seemingly taunted and bullied Emily, more than a decade older than them, because she was tall, thin and ungainly, and because she was reserved and would not answer them back. There were two reasons for the Wheelwrights' attack upon Emily and neither of them had to do with the wide and old-fashioned gigot sleeves that she was mocked for wearing. First, Laetitia doted upon Charlotte and felt that Emily unfairly monopolised her time and company (something that M. Héger also accused Emily of), and second, Emily had started giving piano lessons to the younger Wheelwrights but insisted on giving them at designated play times.

The Hégers had soon noticed Emily's prowess as a pianist, and as well as arranging for a leading piano player and tutor, M. Chapelle, they also employed her services teaching other pupils at the pensionnat. This was part of the deal whereby Charlotte and Emily were permitted to extend their stay beyond the initial half-year, as Charlotte explained in a letter to Ellen:

> I consider it doubtful whether I shall come home in September. Madame Héger has made a proposal for both me and Emily to stay another half-year, offering to dismiss her English master, and take me as English teacher; also to employ Emily some part of each day in teaching music to a certain number of pupils.[11]

This arrangement, eagerly sought by Charlotte, was a terrible blow to Emily, and yet she faced it without flinching, giving her sister little indication that it troubled her. She instead threw herself into her lessons; this is why Emily would only teach piano during leisure periods, so it would not get in the way of her own studies. The move proved deeply unpopular with her pupils, yet she did still manage to make a friend while at the pensionnat in Louise de Bassompierre. Louise was one of her piano pupils, but unlike the frivolous Wheelwrights, she appreciated Emily's seriousness and dedication, recollecting, 'Miss Emily was certainly less brilliant than her sister but much more sympathetic.'[12] Appreciative of the support she received from Louise, Emily presented her with a painting when she left the pensionnat.

Another boon for Emily was that there were two other friendly faces nearby, Mary and Martha Taylor. Although they were primarily friends of Charlotte, they became a welcome sight to Emily too, as simply the sound of their West Riding accents brought back fond memories of home.

The Château de Koekelberg, however, was on the outskirts of Brussels, whereas the Pensionnat Héger was centrally sited, so these invigorating visits to the Taylors came less often than either Emily or Charlotte would have liked. One visit they did undertake on a regular basis, at least initially, was to the home of the English chaplain, Evan Jenkins. Possibly acting on the wishes of Patrick, Reverend Jenkins insisted on the two Brontës going to dine with his family every Sunday at their home on the Chaussée d'Ixelles. It was more than a mile from the school, but rather than letting Emily and Charlotte walk there themselves, which they would doubtless have enjoyed, he instead sent his two sons to escort them. After a number of excruciating weeks, it became apparent that the sisters found the dinners an ordeal, with Charlotte making stilted conversation and Emily not speaking at all. Finally, the invitations stopped, to the relief of both parties.

Back at the school, Charlotte had anticipated Emily finding the lessons very difficult, as they were conducted solely in French and Emily had little prior knowledge of the language. Emily surprised her sister, however, with the dedication she showed to her tuition:

> Emily works like a horse, and she has had great difficulties to contend with, far greater than I have had. Indeed, those who come to a French school for instruction ought previously to have acquired a considerable knowledge of the French language ... for the course of instruction is adapted to natives and not to foreigners.[13]

This same letter also strikes an ominous tone, as Charlotte reports difficulties between her sister and the man whose job it was to teach them the French language, stating, 'Emily and he don't draw well together at all.'[14]

Emily was a woman who had grown used to her own independence, a woman with a distaste for instruction, timetables and discipline. These were all the qualities that Constantin Héger prized most highly, and so it is inevitable that they should have clashed during their first weeks together.

Nevertheless, he persevered with his instruction, giving Emily and Charlotte extra lessons and setting them essays on selected topics rather than making them learn grammar by rote as he did with the younger pupils.

As the weeks progressed, M. Héger's contempt for Emily softened and then turned into admiration. Emily's astonishing mind allowed her to master the French language in a way he could not have anticipated. We have proof of this in Emily's devoirs, the essays that she wrote on the subjects set by her French master. Belying Charlotte's claim of her struggles with French, they are miniature masterpieces, not only of language comprehension but also of thought and creativity.

When asked to write an essay about cats, Emily chose not to talk about their whiskers or how they like to eat fish, but wrote instead about how they resemble man in their hypocrisy and cruelty:

> A cat, in its own interest, sometimes hides its misanthropy under the guise of amiable gentleness; instead of tearing what it desires from its master's hand it approaches with a caressing air, rubs its pretty little head against him, and advances a paw whose touch is as soft as down. When it has gained its end, it resumes its character of Timon; and that artfulness in it is called hypocrisy. In ourselves, we give it another name, politeness, and he who did not use it to hide his real feelings would soon be driven from society.[15]

I have Sue Lonoff to thank for this translation in her book, *The Belgian Essays: A Critical Edition*, but Emily's original is in perfect, masterful French. It was written on 15 May 1842, just three months after her arrival in Brussels, with next to no knowledge of the language, and without access to a dictionary, as that was forbidden by Héger. Emily's devoir on a butterfly takes a similarly philosophical and brilliant turn, as Emily debates the life and death qualities of nature and how the act of killing is central to it:

During my soliloquy I picked a flower at my side; it was fair and freshly opened, but an ugly caterpillar had hidden itself among the petals and already they were shrivelling and fading. 'Sad image of the earth and its inhabitants!' I exclaimed. 'This worm lives only to injure the plant that protects it. Why was it created, and why was man created? He torments, he kills, he devours; he suffers, dies, is devoured – there you have his whole story.'[16]

Emily's devoirs are the only examples of her prose writing that survive other than her novel, and they are astonishing even without taking into account the alien language in which she was writing. They are an early glimpse into an immense and unique mind, a sure indication that had she been able to write further novels after *Wuthering Heights*, they would have been works of great genius.

Constantin Héger could not help but change his opinion of the strange Yorkshire girl's abilities, as he later revealed to Elizabeth Gaskell:

She [Emily] should have been a man – a great navigator. Her powerful reason would have deduced new spheres of discovery from the knowledge of the old; and her strong, imperious will would never have been daunted by opposition or difficulty; never have given way but with life.[17]

Emily was battling homesickness, she was missing Anne and she had ostracised herself from many of her fellow pupils, yet she was learning and she was enduring. Her routine was shaken irrevocably, however, by two tragic events occurring within the space of seventeen days in October 1842.

On 12 October, Martha Taylor died suddenly of cholera. Charlotte especially was devastated; her relationship to Mary's younger sister may never be known, but she had loved her greatly. Martha was recreated as Jessy Yorke in *Shirley*, with her sister Mary as Rose Yorke, and Charlotte uses the novel to pay a mournful tribute to the young woman who had meant so much to her:

> Do you know this place? No, you never saw it; but you recognise the nature of the trees, this foliage – the cypress, the willow, the yew. Stone crosses like these are not unfamiliar to you, nor are these dim garlands of everlasting flowers. Here is the place – green sod and a gray marble headstone. Jessy sleeps below. She lived through an April day; much loved she was, much loving. She often, in her brief life, shed tears, she had frequent sorrows; she smiled between, gladdening whatever saw her ... The dying and the watching English girls were at that hour alone in a foreign country, and the soil of that country gave Jessy a grave.[18]

Martha was indeed buried in the Dissenters' graveyard in Brussels. The graveyard itself has long since been built over, but a tiny memorial to her can be found in the graveyard of St Mary's Church in Gomersal, West Yorkshire. It reads, 'Martha Taylor, much loved she was, much loving. C. Brontë.'

Emily was there to comfort her grieving sister, her unbowed stoicism providing support to Charlotte when she needed it most. However, on 29 October another death came fast on the heels of the first; this time it was at Haworth Parsonage, and it led to Emily's hasty return to England. The weary care was at an end.

WE ARE LEFT BELOW

I do not weep; I would not weep;
Our mother needs no tears:
Dry thine eyes, too; 'tis vain to keep,
This causeless grief for years.
What though her brow be changed and cold,
Her sweet eyes closed for ever?
What though the stone – the darksome mould,
Our mortal bodies sever?
What though her hand smooth ne'er again,
Those silken locks of thine –
Nor through long hours of future pain,
Her kind face o'er thee shine?
Remember still she is not dead;
She sees us Gerald now;
Laid where her angel spirit fled,
'Mid heath and frozen snow.
And from that world of heavenly light,
Will she not always bend,
To guide us in our lifetime's night,
And guard us to the end?

Thou know'st she will; and well may'st mourn,
That we are left below:
But not that she can ne'er return,
To share our earthly woe.

('A.S. to G.S.', dated 19 December 1841)

THE CAUSE OF Emily and Charlotte's rushed return from the Continent was the unexpected death of their aunt, Elizabeth Branwell, the woman who for over twenty years had acted as a second mother to them. The sisters' original plan before their voyage to Brussels was for Anne to return to the parsonage while they were away to take over the duties Emily had been fulfilling, but Anne was held in such high regard by her employers, the Robinsons, that they would not let her leave. Nevertheless, Emily and Charlotte took solace in the seeming good health that their father and aunt were in, so when they left Haworth in February 1842 it was without trepidation.

On Wednesday, 2 November 1842, they received an urgent letter from their father, telling them their aunt had fallen seriously ill. The sisters packed their belongings immediately and explained the situation to the Hégers, as they planned the journey back to England. The next day, they received another letter informing them of their aunt's death. It had actually happened five days before the first letter reached the Pensionnat Héger, but Emily and Charlotte agreed that they must return to England to pay their final respects.

They arrived in Haworth on 8 November, nine months to the day after they had set out on their adventure. Charlotte, after an interval of nearly three months, returned to Brussels, but Emily now insisted on staying in Haworth and resuming her former role. For Charlotte, this second spell in Brussels proved to be sad and disheartening, increasingly obsessed as she was with Constantin Héger, irritated by her pupils, and without Emily to console her and provide common-sense advice at the end of the day. Nevertheless, the influence Brussels had on Charlotte is plain to see as it forms the backdrop to two of her novels, *The Professor* and *Villette*, as well as providing an event in *Shirley* and a protagonist in *Jane Eyre*.

Some commentators have said that the months spent in Brussels had no impact on Emily, but the fact she did not write about them directly does not diminish the importance they had in her life and her writing. The nine months spent in Belgium allowed Emily to exorcise her most powerful demon; she had proved to her fiercest critic – herself – that she could survive away from home and successfully mix with other people, to a degree at least. She was no longer the homesick girl of Roe Head, she was a strong woman who could overcome adversity with the sheer force of her will.

The change this brought in her life was perhaps unexpected, in that rather than developing a taste for social interaction she became even more insular: after all, she had proved to her own satisfaction that she could survive in the outer world if she had to, why do it again? From this point on, Emily rarely left Haworth other than on her daily walks across the moors, and the only journeys she took in the final six years of her life were to York with Anne and Manchester with Charlotte as they sought advice over a potential cataract operation for their father.[1] Visitors to the parsonage who were unknown to her would remain unknown. Emily made no effort to get to know them or even to be civil to them, as this recollection of Ellen Nussey shows: 'It used to be a matter of surprise to Charlotte that she [Emily] made an exception in my favour – she used to wish for my visits and was always kind and polite in her behaviour, which was not often the case to other guests.'[2]

The impact of Brussels upon Emily's writing has been unfairly downplayed – after all, we should remember that she was an arch-observer of people and so her months there would have afforded her countless memories of human behaviour that would eventually find their way, disguised, into print. The impact of the woman who paid for Emily's departure to Belgium and whose death led to her return has also been undervalued. One of the obvious characteristics of *Wuthering Heights* is the strong women in it, from haughty

Cathy to the dependable Nellie Dean; this is a tribute to the impact that women had in Emily's life, not only her sisters, but also Aunt Branwell and Tabby Aykroyd.

Elizabeth Branwell was born in 1776, in Penzance near the far south-western tip of England, the sixth child born to Thomas Branwell and Anne Carne, who would eventually have eleven children, not all of whom survived infancy. Their house at 25 Chapel Street in Penzance still stands today, a moderately large brick-faced building made of granite. Nearby is the beautiful old town with rustic medieval cottages and the famous Admiral Benbow Inn (unlikely to have been favoured by the Branwells, given their Methodism which placed an emphasis upon temperance). A short walk from the house are the golden sands of the beach, and not far across the sea lies the ever-visible glory of St Michael's Mount.

On the Chapel Street building sits a plaque in memory of the two women of note who grew up there: 'This was the home of Maria and Elizabeth Branwell, the mother and aunt of Charlotte, Emily, Anne and Branwell Brontë.' It is a pleasant house, but it gives little indication of the comfort in which the family within it lived. The Branwells were a wealthy and powerful family in southern Cornwall. Elizabeth's father Thomas was a grocer and seller of fine teas, with retail premises on Market Square and warehouses on the docks. He also owned a number of properties in and around Penzance, including the Golden Lion Inn and the large Tremenheere House. His wife Anne was from a successful family too, with her father a silversmith and her brother William the founder of the Penzance Bank in 1797.

Elizabeth grew up without knowing want, in a happy and growing family. When she was 6 or 7, she gained another sister, Maria, the eighth child of Thomas and Anne. From an early age they became close, and it seems the Branwell family as a whole was close. Elizabeth never married as her siblings who lived to adulthood did, but she was renowned as a sensible and dependable member of the family, acting as witness to the marriage of her brother and sisters. The Branwell children were also close to their Aunt Jane, who married the Reverend John Fennell, an act that proved very significant in the Brontë story.

The Branwells were a highly religious family, renowned for their support of the Methodist cause. Methodism was particularly popular in the south-west of England, with the Wesley brothers frequently preaching there. Thomas was one of the main financial backers of the construction of the first Methodist church in Penzance, completed in 1814,[3] and Elizabeth would have taken pride of place in the front pews.

The religious conviction of the Branwell children is demonstrated by a treatise that Maria wrote entitled 'The Advantages of Poverty in Religious Concerns'.[4] Despite their belief in the spiritual riches of poverty, the Branwells' daily life also included grand dinners, music recitals and society balls. As an indication of their standing in Penzance society, Elizabeth and Maria's older brother, Benjamin Carne Branwell, became the town's mayor in 1809,[5] succeeding Thomas Giddy in the post. However, then a double tragedy hit the family that would see the children separated one from another.

Thomas Branwell died in 1808 and his wife Anne just a year later. The family home on Chapel Street was inherited, not as may be expected by his son Benjamin but by his brother Richard, who ran Thomas' Golden Lion Inn. The loss of both parents in such a short space of time must have been hard for Elizabeth to take, but at least her domestic situation continued largely unchanged, as Richard allowed his nieces Maria, Elizabeth and Charlotte to continue living there. They also had an annuity of £50 from their father's will to support them.[6]

Things changed irrevocably in 1812, after another double tragedy in the family. In late 1811, Maria and Elizabeth's cousin Thomas, son of Richard and a dashing naval officer, drowned aboard the *St George*. A heartbroken Richard died a few months later, and it could be that this threw ownership of the Branwell properties into doubt, as Charlotte soon afterwards married her cousin Joseph Branwell, another of Richard's sons, with Maria also leaving for new horizons.

Maria Branwell, as we know, made the long journey northwards to join her Aunt Jane at Woodhouse Grove School near Leeds, where she would soon meet and marry Patrick Brontë. Only Elizabeth was left now, alone with memories of the large, thriving family to which she had once belonged. It was a scenario that would be repeated by her niece Charlotte Brontë four decades later, although in rather different circumstances.

It is thought that Elizabeth Branwell may have lived for a time with her sister Charlotte and brother-in-law Joseph in Cornwall, but in 1815 she too made the journey north to Yorkshire. She arrived in Thornton in 1815, helping her sister Maria settle into the new parish and the life of a new mother to daughters, Maria and Elizabeth. Elizabeth Branwell remained in Thornton for just over a year, returning to Cornwall in 1816. Little was she to know that just five years later she would be making a permanent home in Yorkshire's West Riding.

Elizabeth must have kept up a correspondence with her sister in Yorkshire, for in 1821 she discovered that Maria had fallen dreadfully ill in her husband's new parish of Haworth. It is likely that this letter was sent by Patrick, and upon its receipt she did not hesitate: her place was at the side of the sister she loved like no other. Elizabeth arrived at Haworth Parsonage in May 1821, and she found her sister dying and a house filled with six children. Four terrible months later, poor Maria's suffering came to an end, and it was now that Elizabeth, or Aunt Branwell as she had already become known, showed her true spirit and character.

Penzance is as distant from Haworth as is Brussels, later visited by Emily and Charlotte. Haworth's landscape was alien to Elizabeth, as were the customs and accents of the people she found around her. The climate was perhaps the greatest challenge she faced, leaving the year-round warmth of Cornwall for the cold, wuthering weather of the Pennine moors. She was particularly distressed by the draughts blowing between flagstones in the parsonage, which is why she wore the overshoes known as pattens, even when she was indoors. It was one of the many peculiarities in her dress noted by visitors, as they reported to Elizabeth Gaskell: 'I have heard that Miss Branwell always went about the house in pattens, clicking up and down the stairs, from her dread of catching cold.'[7]

In spite of all this, she left behind the comfortable world of Penzance for a colder, uncertain future in Yorkshire. Aunt Branwell did not flinch; she was determined to raise her nephew and nieces as she thought her sister would have wanted, and in doing so, at the age of 45, she sacrificed everything, including any lingering hope she may have had of finding a husband herself.

Aunt Branwell now saw her main role as raising her six new charges to be well behaved, well disciplined, and God-fearing. She read to them from scripture, and also made them sew for hours at a time. This was a practical expediency for their present as well as the future, as the Brontë children typically had to repair their clothing until it could be repaired no more. This has led some to view Elizabeth Branwell as a strict, unbending, almost uncaring figure, but this is as unfair as the verdict Mrs Gaskell passed upon her: 'The children respected her, and had that sort of affection for her which is generated by esteem; but I do not think they ever freely loved her.'[8]

This could be the verdict of Charlotte, who may have been disconcerted by her aunt's favouritism of her youngest sister, but it was certainly not the view of Anne or Branwell. Elizabeth was as a mother to Anne, and the niece's affection for her aunt is shown in this passage from *Agnes Grey*:

In my childhood I could not imagine a more afflictive punishment than for my mother to refuse to kiss me at night: the very idea was terrible. More than the idea I never felt, for, happily, I never committed a fault that was deemed worthy of such penalty; but once I remember, for some transgression of my sister's, our mother thought proper to inflict it upon her: what *she* felt, I cannot tell; but my sympathetic tears and suffering for her sake I shall not soon forget.[9]

Like much of *Agnes Grey*, this is based upon Anne's life, with the 'mother' of the novel representing Aunt Branwell rather than the actual mother who had died in Anne's infancy. It is not too much of a leap to imagine that the sister being punished was the headstrong Emily, but Ellen Nussey recalled another side to her:

Miss Branwell was a very small, antiquated little lady. She wore caps large enough for half a dozen of the present fashion, and in front of light auburn curls over her forehead. She always dressed in silk. She had a horror of the climate so far north, and of the stone floors in the parsonage ... She talked a great deal of her younger days; the gaieties of her dear native town Penzance ... she gave one the idea that she had been a belle among her home acquaintants. She took snuff out of a very pretty gold snuff-box, which she sometimes presented to you with a little laugh, as if she enjoyed the slight shock and astonishment visible in your countenance ... She and Mr Brontë had often to finish their discussions on what she had read when we all met for tea. She would be very lively and intelligent, and tilt arguments against Mr Brontë without fear.[10]

This is a very different picture from the one painted by Mrs Gaskell who, after all, never met Elizabeth Branwell. Now we see an intelligent woman, not afraid to argue her point with Patrick Brontë, creating mutual admiration between them in the process. We see a woman who has a rather formal front, but is actually fond of playing wicked tricks on people and then laughing. These are characteristics that were also to be found in her niece Emily.

Perhaps the greatest thing that she did for Emily, and for Charlotte and Anne, was to encourage their reading and learning. It was she who bought them the gift of Sir Walter Scott's *Tales of a Grandfather* in 1828; a thoughtful gift that shows how well she understood her nieces' tastes and one that would spark a lifelong love of Scott in Emily in particular, as is plain in *Wuthering Heights*.

Aunt Branwell created the security the Brontës needed more than anything else and provided them with the love of a mother as best she could. It may often have been a formal love typical of the early nineteenth century, and of the century before from which she hailed, but it was a love nonetheless. It was she who set house rules, set homework and domestic tasks, but it was also she who accompanied them to and from concerts as children (Patrick was a creature of habit and would always insist upon leaving punctually at 9, on his own). She also made generous financial contributions to help her sister's children. We know that she paid for Emily and Charlotte to go to Brussels, and it is likely that she had earlier paid for Branwell to visit London, and that she contributed to the purchase of the piano and music lessons.

She was a figure of stability in Emily's life for twenty-one years from the moment she walked, with a shiver, through the parsonage door in 1821. Despite her fear of colds and a distaste for exercise, she enjoyed almost uniformly good health until, on 25 October 1842, she suffered a strangulation of the bowel from which she died four painful days later. Emily's poem, although written a year earlier, shows how she would have reacted. She would not weep openly for her aunt – after all, she did not suffer as those who had to live suffered. There is no doubt, however, that Emily felt her loss deeply.

An indication of the true manner in which the Brontë children regarded her, and the depth of pain her loss caused them, is revealed by what some would think an unlikely source: Elizabeth's nephew, Branwell. She had grown close to her sister's only son, despite his failings and weaknesses. She did not approve of his drinking, or later of his drug-taking, but nor did she judge him beyond help, and nor did she cut him off or abandon him. After her death, Branwell paid his aunt a touching and fitting tribute in two letters to his friend Francis Grundy: 'I am attending at the death-bed of my aunt, who has been for twenty years as my mother. I expect her to die in a few hours.'[11] His subsequent letter after her death was the despairing missive of a son who has lost his much-loved mother:

I am incoherent, I fear, but I have been waking two nights witnessing such agonising suffering as I would not wish my worst enemy to endure; and I have now lost the guide and director of all the happy days connected with my childhood.[12]

Aunt Branwell left Emily and her siblings a legacy of love from her life in the parsonage, but she left them a financial legacy too. This windfall freed the Brontë sisters from immediate money worries, and led directly to the sequence of books that would astonish the world.

ON A STRANGE ROAD

Oh, thy bright eyes must answer now,
When Reason, with a scornful brow,
Is mocking at my overthrow!
Oh, thy sweet tongue must plead for me,
And tell, why I have chosen thee!
Stern Reason is to judgment come,
Arrayed in all her forms of gloom:
Wilt thou, my advocate, be dumb?
No, radiant angel, speak and say,
Why I did cast the world away.
Why I have persevered to shun,
The common paths that others run,
And on a strange road journeyed on,
Heedless alike, of wealth and power –
Of glory's wreath and pleasure's flower.
These, once indeed, seemed Beings Divine;
And they, perchance, heard vows of mine,
And saw my offerings on their shrine;
But, careless gifts are seldom prized,
And *mine* were worthily despised.
So with a ready heart I swore,

To seek their altar-stone no more;
And gave my spirit to adore,
Thee, ever present, phantom thing;
My slave, my comrade, and my King,
A slave, because I rule thee still;
Incline thee to my changeful will,
And make thy influence good or ill;
A comrade, for by day and night,
Thou art my intimate delight, –
My darling pain that wounds and sears,
And wrings a blessing out from tears,
By deadening me to earthly cares;
And yet, a king, though Prudence well,
Have taught thy subject to rebel.
And am I wrong to worship, where,
Faith cannot doubt, nor Hope despair,
Since my own soul can grant my prayer?
Speak, God of visions, plead for me,
And tell why I have chosen thee!

('Plead for Me', dated 14 October 1844)

AS THIS BRILLIANT and revelatory poem shows, by late 1844 Emily Brontë had firmly prioritised the land of creativity and imagination over any notion of life outside Haworth's parsonage and moors. The visionary experiences that had come to her since childhood were now both her king, because she longed for them more than anything else, and her slave, because she could control them in a way that had been out of reach in her younger days. With increasingly powerful visions came increasingly powerful writing. It was revelatory writing, revealing Emily's true feelings, beliefs and emotions, and for that reason she kept it a closely guarded secret, even from her sisters. It was intended to be writing that would never be seen by human eyes, but a chance discovery and the contents of her aunt's will ensured that the writing, and Emily herself, received a very different fate.

Aunt Branwell died in October 1842, but she was a woman who believed in the importance of planning and preparation and so had made her will on 30 April 1833, with her brother-in-law Patrick serving as executor alongside George Taylor. The will begins by leaving some of her much-loved personal items, brought from Penzance, to her nieces, including 'My workbox with a China top I leave to my niece Emily Jane Brontë, together with my ivory fan'.[1] After leaving the sum of £25 to her sister Jane Kingston, she leaves the rest 'To accumulate for the sole benefit of my four nieces, Charlotte Brontë, Emily Jane Brontë, Anne Brontë, and Elizabeth Jane Kingston'.[2]

The will is a good indication not only of Elizabeth Branwell's esteem for the nieces she was raising, but also of her kind-heartedness and intelligence. She knew that, out of all her siblings, it was her sister Jane who was in most need. Jane Branwell had married a Methodist preacher called John Kingston and emigrated to America. It was a deeply unhappy marriage and she returned to Cornwall with her youngest child Elizabeth, leaving her older children in America with their father. It was a despairing move and brought with it many difficulties, which is why Aunt Branwell left both Jane and Elizabeth Kingston a legacy in her will. It should be noted here that the omission of Elizabeth's nephew Branwell Brontë from her will was not a slight against a boy she had grown fond of. At the time the will was made, Branwell was 15 years of age and his aunt had an expectation that he would become a great success in whatever career lay ahead of him, meaning he would have no need of the financial support that would surely help his sisters.

The three sisters and their cousin Elizabeth Jane Kingston each received a sum of around £300. This was a significant amount, which has a basic equivalence of between £225,000 and £366,000 today (according to the 'measuring worth' website that calculates modern values using labour earnings and economic status, as well as the basic inflationary rise).[3] This windfall alleviated their immediate concerns about securing enough money to live on, which proved timely as less than two years later all four Brontë children were out of work and back under the familiar roof of Haworth Parsonage.

The circumstances that brought Emily home from Brussels were mournful, but the result was liberating. Emily returned to baking the bread, cleaning the house, learning German when and where she wanted, walking the moors and composing poetry, just as she had a year before. The cloud of homesickness drifted away, and she was once again in the environment she loved more than any other.

In this familiar routine, Emily passed a happy 1843 with Charlotte serving as a teacher once more in Brussels, and Anne and Branwell, newly appointed after the recommendation of his sister, serving as governess and governor at Thorp Green Hall near York. This domestic stability was not to last.

In the first week of 1844, Charlotte arrived back in Haworth having left Brussels for the final time. She had in her hands a diploma from the Athénée Royal, the boys' school headed by M. Héger, testifying to her ability in the French language and her experience as a teacher, and in her heart a growing, numbing coldness.[4] At least she now had the support of her ever-dependable Emily, whose calm advice had been so sorely missed over the previous year of love and despair. By the summer of 1845, Emily's expertise as a silent comforter was in high demand, as Anne and Branwell were also back in the parsonage, but for very different reasons.

Anne was a firm believer in the ability of people to change, and she was confident that the job she had secured for her brother would be the making of him; the discipline and ordered routine would help him overcome his sorrows and addictions, and in doing so he could regain his self-respect at the same time as earning money for himself. We all know, of course, that Anne's reasoning in this instance was completely wrong. Branwell soon fell in love with Lydia Robinson, mistress of Thorp Green Hall, and if Branwell's reports are to be believed, his feelings were reciprocated.

Anne was shocked by this turn of events, later recalling, 'I have had some very unpleasant and undreamt-of experience of human nature.'[5] By June 1845 she could take no more, and resigned her post. A month later, possibly having grown bolder without Anne's presence to regulate his behaviour, Branwell's behaviour was discovered and he was dismissed. The Brontës were united in Haworth once again. They were now aged between 25 and 29, with no employment and few prospects ahead of them.

This could have been a time to resurrect their plan for a school which, after all, had been the supposed reason for Charlotte and Emily's sojourn in Brussels, but this once-cherished idea was by now a dead dream. After Charlotte's return to Haworth in January 1844, the sisters decided to modify their plan and open a small school within Haworth Parsonage itself. Changes would need to be made to the building, but they had their aunt's legacy to cover that so, undaunted, they had a prospectus printed that was headed, 'The Misses Brontës' Establishment for the Board and Education of a Limited Number of Young Ladies'. There was no lack of effort, but no pupils were secured, with the only offer coming from M. Héger, who had proposed sending one of his own daughters to the school.[6]

There were many factors against its success: the basic and rather high fee of £35 per year, the remoteness of Haworth and its unhealthy reputation, and the unpredictable presence of Branwell in the house. Emily summed up her attitude to the demise of the scheme in her 1845 diary paper:

I should have mentioned that last summer the school scheme was revived in full vigour – we had prospectuses printed, despatched letters to all acquaintances imparting our plans and did our little all – but it was found no go. Now I don't desire a school at all and none of us have any great longing for it.[7]

Emily's enthusiasm for the school was never strong after her initial flourish had faded, and even before the scheme was abandoned her potential role had been downgraded, as Charlotte revealed in a letter to M. Héger:

Emily does not like teaching much, but she would always do the housekeeping and, although she is a little reclusive, she has too good a heart not to do everything for the wellbeing of the children.[8]

By late 1844 it was obvious that the Brontë school would never open to the public, making Anne's resignation the following year an ominous portent for their futures. They had all tried and failed, to a greater or lesser extent, to make a career for themselves; their father was getting older and was nearly blind; and there did not even seem to be the possibility of marriage for the sisters (even though none of them would have been open to a proposal anyway). Emily, at least, was happy with this turn of events, but Charlotte and Anne had reached a nadir in their lives, which was behind Anne's proclamation, 'I for my part cannot well be flatter or older in mind than I am now.'[9]

Anne's despondent cry was committed to paper in July 1845, but two months later an unexpected event gave her and Charlotte hope, at the same time turning Emily's tranquillity into torment. Charlotte gave her explanation of what happened in the 1850 biographical notice of her sisters:

> One day, in the autumn of 1845, I accidentally lighted on a manuscript volume of verse in my sister Emily's handwriting. Of course, I was not surprised, knowing that she could and did write verse: I looked it over, and something more than surprise seized me, – a deep conviction that these were not common effusions, nor at all like the poetry women generally write. I thought them condensed and terse, vigorous and genuine. To my ear, they also had a peculiar music – wild, melancholy, and elevating.[10]

This was not the Gondal notebook that is now in the British Library, containing poems that Emily freely shared with her sisters, but something altogether different. Emily's secret, vision-inspired poetry was for her eyes alone; it contained the keys to her very soul, and when she found that Charlotte had discovered and read it she was plunged into a red-misted despair. The intensely shy Emily had had her covers torn away, exposing her innermost thoughts and desires and, even worse, Charlotte now wanted her to expose these most private compositions to the world, to be judged by whoever would pay to see them. Charlotte insisted that they were too good to be locked away.

It was more than Emily could bear. Her shrieks of anger pierced the air and papers and ornaments were sent flying. For two days Emily raged and wept, leaving her sisters worried for her health, until at last she showed signs of the return of reason. It was then that Anne diffused the situation by presenting her poems as well, and suggesting that they could all three submit their poetry to be printed together.

Emily was placed into what was, for her, the most dreadful dilemma. Could she bring herself to show her personal poems to the world? To do so would go against all her beliefs and principles, but if she did not she would be denying Anne, the sister she loved, the chance to see her own work in print. Charlotte, still wary of another outburst, soothed Emily by reminding her of the times they had written together as children, suggesting that this new project would unite them in the same way.

Emily very reluctantly agreed, but on the strict condition that her true identity be hidden: this was the birth of Currer, Ellis and Acton Bell. Male pseudonyms were adopted to overcome the prejudice that all three sisters felt was levelled against women writers. The surname Bell may have been borrowed from new assistant curate, Arthur Bell Nicholls, later to be Charlotte's husband, but where did the first names come from? Charlotte's Currer is inspired by Frances Currer of Eshton Hall, near Skipton, whom Charlotte could have met when she was a governess at neighbouring Stone Gappe. Anne's Acton is probably a tribute to Eliza Acton, a popular female poet of the early nineteenth century. Emily's Ellis could have been inspired by Ellis Cunliffe Lister, Member of Parliament for nearby Bradford, whose daughter Mary had been Anne's employer at Blake Hall. I like to think, however, that it was a tribute to Elizabeth Brontë, the kind, practical and tragic elder sister whom Emily never forgot.

The tension between Emily and Charlotte took a long time to heal, and even today we are left wondering if Charlotte did accidentally light upon the manuscript as she said, or if she had prised it from a hiding place. Whatever the truth, the act of collating the collection marked the start of the healing process. It was decided that Emily and Anne would contribute twenty-one poems each, with Charlotte contributing nineteen, as hers were typically much longer compositions (although she must also have known that her two sisters' poetry was of a higher standard).

Emily's poetry is, without doubt, the highlight of the collection that became known as *Poems by Currer, Ellis and Acton Bell*. The poems of the sisters are mainly alternated throughout the volume, and Emily's first contribution is 'Faith and Despondency', which headed Chapter 4 of this book. Among Ellis Bell's timeless gems in the collection are 'The Philosopher', 'The Prisoner', 'My Comforter', and the verse at the top of this chapter, 'Plead for Me'. Contemporary readers must have been astonished not only at the beautiful rhythms of these poems, but also by their wild symbolism, full of visions and magic. Unfortunately, very few contemporary readers saw them.

Once Emily's anger had subsided, a process that must have taken weeks, if not months, she felt some excitement at the prospect of seeing their work in print, just as they had already seen their father's work in print on his bookshelves. The first problem they encountered was finding a publisher. After a series of rejection letters, one publisher recommended to the Bells a specialist poetry press called Aylott & Jones, of London. Aylott & Jones agreed to publish the poetry, but on the proviso that the poets themselves would have to pay the upfront costs, adding up to a substantial £31 10*s*.[11]

If this offer had come four years earlier, it would have been beyond the Brontës' means and it is likely that we would never have seen any of their work in print. Now, at the beginning of 1846, they had their aunt's legacy to fund their venture. We can guess their reasoning: the money would not be used for a school, so why not use it to fund their poetry? After all, they had absolutely no other prospective means of making money.

Poems by Currer, Ellis and Acton Bell was published in May 1846, and it attracted relatively positive reviews from publications including *The Critic* and *The Athenaeum*. Good reviews did not equal good sales, however, and a miserly two copies were initially sold. The sisters were not disheartened, as Charlotte's jocular letter to the writer Thomas de Quincey, with an enclosed copy of the book, shows:

> My relatives, Ellis and Acton Bell and myself, heedless of the repeated warnings of various respectable publishers, have committed the rash act of publishing a volume of poems. The consequences predicted have, of course, overtaken us; our book is found to be a drug; no man needs it or heeds it; in the space of a year our publisher has disposed of but two copies, and by what painful efforts he succeeded in disposing of those two, himself only knows.[12]

Less well known is that in 1848, the publisher Smith, Elder & Co. bought up all unsold copies of the work from Aylott & Jones, rebound them and succeeded in selling every one.[13]

Even so, Charlotte and Anne must initially have viewed this speculation as a failure, even if Emily may secretly have been glad that only two people had seen her poetry and unconcerned that her careless gifts had been so seldom prized. It was of little consequence when compared to what happened next. The Brontë sisters, under the masks of the Bell brothers, had rediscovered their love of writing together. Poetry was put aside; it was now time to assemble a prose collection. It was time for *Wuthering Heights*.

16

VAIN, FRENZIED
THOUGHTS

Light up thy halls! 'Tis closing day;
I'm drear and lone and far away –
Cold blows on my breast, the north wind's bitter sigh,
And oh, my couch is bleak beneath the rainy sky!
Light up thy halls – and think not of me;
That face is absent now, thou hast hated so to see –
Bright be thine eyes, undimmed their dazzling shine,
For never, never more shall they encounter mine!
The desert moor is dark; there is tempest in the air;
I have breathed my only wish in one last, one burning prayer –
A prayer that would come forth although it lingered long;
That set on fire my heart, but froze upon my tongue –
And now, it shall be done before the morning rise;
I will not watch the sun ascend in yonder skies.
One task alone remains – thy pictured face to view,
And then I go to prove if God, at least, be true!
Do I not see thee now? Thy black resplendent hair;
The glory-beaming brow, and smile how heavenly fair!
Thine eyes are turned away – those eyes I would not see;

Their dark, their deadly ray would more than madden me.
Then, go, Deceiver, go! My hair is streaming wet,
My heart's blood flows to buy the blessing – To forget!
Oh could that lost heart give back, back again to thine,
One tenth part of the pain that clouds my dark decline!
Oh could I see thy lids weighed down in cheerless woe;
Too full to hide their tears, too stern to overflow;
Oh could I know thy soul with equal grief was torn,
This fate might be endured – this anguish might be borne!
How gloomy grows the Night! 'Tis Gondal's wind that blows,
I shall not tread again the deep glens where it rose –
I feel it on my face – Where, wild blast, dost thou roam?
What do we, wanderer, here, so far away from home?
I do not need thy breath to cool my death-cold brow,
But go to that far land, where she is shining now;
Tell Her my latest wish, tell Her my dreary doom;
Say, that *my* pangs are past, but Hers are yet to come –
Vain words – vain, frenzied thoughts! No ear can hear me call –
Lost in the vacant air my frantic curses fall,
And could she see me now, perchance her lip would smile,
Would smile in careless pride and utter scorn the while!
And yet, for all her hate, each parting glance would tell,
A stronger passion breathed, burned in this last farewell –
Unconquered in my soul the Tyrant rules me still –
Life bows to my control, but, *Love* I cannot kill!

('F. De Samara to A.G.A.', dated 1 November 1838)

B Y THE AGE of 20, Emily Brontë's Gondal poems had reached their passionate, dramatic height, as this dark and fiery example shows. It is a wild and melancholy poem, mixed with spite and yearning, and central to it is a theme that Emily would turn to once more when she came to write her only novel, seven years later.

Fernando de Samara is a nobleman from the land of Exina who has fallen in love with Augusta Geraldine Almeida, the temperamental Queen of Gondal with a string of conquests to her name. They embark upon an affair as destructive as it is cruel; Augusta eventually imprisons Fernando within a dungeon deep in the Gaaldine Caves. As this poem opens, Fernando has escaped his earthly prison, but realises that he cannot escape the prison of his heart. Augusta has a tyrant's power over him, and the only release he will ever have from his overbearing love is death. As night falls, Fernando gazes upon a picture of his conqueror, and then takes his own life.

Fernando, the man who has a despotic power over others and yet is brought low by his love for a woman who is pledged to another, is a prototype Heathcliff, and this poem shows how Emily had been thinking about themes that would appear in *Wuthering Heights* since childhood. Emily's own Gondal poetry was just one of a number of influences that shaped her novel, and as 1845 turned into 1846 they came together to create an astonishing masterpiece.

As a child and teenager Emily had loved nothing more than walking round and round the Haworth Parsonage dining table, a table upon which can still be seen the letter 'E' that she (presumably) scratched into it, composing poems and stories. The months of 1845 spent collating and debating their poems had resurrected those days in Emily's mind, so that she even, for a while, forgot the injury she had felt at the discovery of her hidden poems. Branwell was a lost cause, and it was now painfully obvious that he could play no part in their new writing endeavours, but the renewal of the activity that brought them so much joy in childhood elated Emily, Charlotte and Anne almost as much in adulthood.

As if knowing how little time they had left, as soon as they had finished collecting their poetry the Brontës embarked upon a new and even more adventurous scheme, as Charlotte recalled in 1850:

> Ill-success failed to crush us: the mere effort to succeed had given a wonderful zest to existence; it must be pursued. We each set to work on a prose tale: Ellis Bell produced *Wuthering Heights*, Acton Bell *Agnes Grey*, and Currer Bell also wrote a narrative in one volume.[1]

While Charlotte's recollection of sentiment may be accurate, the timing she refers to is rather less so, for, in fact, work upon the novels started before their poems had even found a publisher, at a time when they were still hopeful of the collection's success. The sisters were aware, however, that the golden age of poetry was over, and that novels were now a much more commercial proposition, as the plethora of adverts within *Blackwood's Magazine* showed. They were also aware that one format in particular sold well: the three-volume novel, or 'triple decker'.

Books were an expensive, if popular, commodity in the first half of the nineteenth century, so many people borrowed them from circulating libraries rather than buying. By publishing books in three volumes, the publisher could make three times as much money from the libraries that purchased them. This led to the clever strategy adopted by Emily and her sisters: they would write a one-volume story each, which could then be published together in a three-volume set.

Emily was much happier with this arrangement than she was with the publication of her poetry, as she could now write a novel that contained all the excitement of her Gondal stories but did not reveal her innermost feelings and beliefs as her poetry had. By mid-1846, the three volumes, still bearing the pseudonyms of the Bell brothers, were finished and making their way to publishers for their consideration. The first publisher approached, reasonably enough, was Aylott & Jones, which was then in the process of launching *Poems by Currer, Ellis and Acton Bell*:

> C., E. & A. Bell are now preparing for the Press a work of fiction – consisting of three distinct and unconnected tales which may be published either together as a work of 3 vols. of the ordinary novel-size, or separately as single vols – as shall be deemed most advisable. It is not their intention to publish these tales on their own account.[2]

Aylott & Jones wrote back explaining that, as they only published poetry, the series of novels would be unsuited to them. They also, however, supplied a list of potential publishers who could be interested, and it was this list that they began to work their way down. At first there seemed little interest in the Bell brothers' novels, and their cause probably wasn't helped by them using the same packaging with the address of the previous recipient scribbled out.

Things were looking bleak for the sisters' writing careers, as terse rejection letters followed one upon another, and by now it had also become obvious that their poetry had proved far from popular. This was a real blow to Charlotte and Anne, but Emily bore it in typically stoic fashion; after all, she could always continue with her routine as unpaid housekeeper at Haworth Parsonage and, as she said in her 1845 diary paper when reporting the failure of their school plans, 'We have cash enough for our present wants with a prospect of accumulation … merely desiring that everybody could be as comfortable as myself and as undesponding and then we should have a very tolerable world of it.'[3]

Emily was referring here to the windfall from their aunt's will, and the prospect that shares they had invested in would prosper. Emily, in tribute to her sensible attitude and calm reasoning, had been put in charge of investing some of their money in railway shares. It was a booming industry, but also a risky one, and eventually the Brontës lost their investment.

Better news arrived in July 1846, at least for two of the sisters. Charlotte opened a letter and discovered that Thomas Cautley Newby & Sons of London were prepared to publish *Wuthering Heights* and *Agnes Grey*. Charlotte's novel *The Professor* was not wanted, but she continued to send it to every name on the list of publishers, until it became obvious even to her that it was unloved and unheeded. The rejected novel, about an Englishman who moves to Belgium, becomes a teacher, and falls in love with a student, was eventually published posthumously, but many of the themes in the novel were used much more successfully (but with the roles reversed) in Charlotte's final novel *Villette*.

This was a blow for Charlotte, who had now seen her two younger sisters usurp her dream to be a writer. It was, of course, one she would recover from spectacularly by penning *Jane Eyre*, but at the time she must have envisaged a future with Emily and Anne as writers, while she was left at home or toiling again as a governess. Charlotte preached caution to her sisters, pointing out that they had agreed not to pay for publication on this occasion, as they had with their poems, whereas Newby was asking for an advance sum of £50, which he promised to repay when they had recouped that amount in sales.

It was a pivotal moment in Emily's life; she had earlier acquiesced to the poetry plan against her better judgement, but this time she would not allow her elder sister's wishes to override her own. Emily knew what she had written was special, and hidden securely behind the pen name of Ellis Bell she had few qualms about sending it before the world. With enough funds from Aunt Branwell's legacy still available, she insisted that she would accept the offer from Thomas Newby, and her sister Anne was quick to concur.

Wuthering Heights is a book that was a handful of months in the writing, but which had been a lifetime in the planning. It is full of influences from Emily's reading matter and from her life, with perhaps the first prototype of Heathcliff leaping, not from a page but from the stories she had heard of her own ancestor, Welsh Brunty. Welsh, as we found in Chapter 1, was a foundling raised by the Brunty family, but his erratic behaviour almost brought ruin to them – especially after he married one of the Brunty daughters in secret and then adopted a nephew. This nephew, a real-life Hareton, was of course Emily's own grandfather, Hugh.

A similar tale of revenge and usurpation is also closely linked to *Wuthering Heights*, and shows the true importance of the months Emily spent in Halifax. While she was a teacher at Law Hill she would undoubtedly have heard of the recent, and very strange, history of the building. Less than a mile from Law Hill stands Walterclough Hall, which had been home to the Walker family since the sixteenth century. In the early eighteenth century, the head of the household was wealthy corn merchant John Walker, whose eldest son, another John, was at Cambridge University. Upon his sister Anne Sharp's death, Walker adopted her nephew Jack Sharp and brought him to live with him at Walterclough Hall.

He found Jack a forceful and manipulative character, so that by 1758 he decided that his only chance of escaping his nephew's influence was to leave his family home and retire to York. Jack Sharp was left with the hall and the lucrative family business, leaving the presumptive heir, John Walker, now back from Cambridge, in effect disinherited. This all changed when John married a woman named Elizabeth Waddington, who insisted that he regain Walterclough Hall for them to live in as a married couple.

Sharp had no option but to move out, but before doing so he destroyed the interior of Walterclough Hall, taking all that he could, and building his own home in the near vicinity. To add to this revenge, he took as his apprentice a much-loved cousin of John Walker called Sam Stead, and promptly taught him to be as evil and feckless as possible, in the same way that Heathcliff corrupts Hareton. Jack Sharp eventually, inevitably, became bankrupt, but escaped to a new life in London. Sam Stead was then taken into Walterclough Hall, but he in turn instructed the Walkers' young son to swear and argue. This real-life story is in many ways a facsimile of *Wuthering Heights* – and the name of the building Jack Sharp built, and from which he plotted his revenge on the Walkers? It was Law Hill which, a century later, became the school at which Emily served,[4] and where one of her fellow teachers was Mrs Earnshaw.

Emily's months at Halifax not only shaped the novel *Wuthering Heights*, they also shaped the fictional building of the same name as well, as the town's High Sunderland Hall is often cited as the origin of Heathcliff's once-grand farmhouse.[5] Although long since demolished, High Sunderland had engravings that call to mind Lockwood's description:

> Before passing the threshold I paused to admire a quantity of grotesque carving lashed over the front, and especially about the principal door, above which, among a wilderness of crumbling griffins, and shameless little boys, I detected the date '1500' and the name 'Hareton Earnshaw'.[6]

High Sunderland is one of three buildings that can be said to have influenced the eponymous building in Emily's novel. Another is Ponden Hall, a place we know Emily visited frequently and where she stayed in a box bed with a window looking out onto the moors, just like the one used by Lockwood before he is roused by the spectre of Cathy. The building most often associated with Wuthering Heights is Top Withens. Once a stone shepherd's hut, and now little more than a ruin, it is a site of pilgrimage for Brontë lovers today. Top Withens represents the location of the Heights most admirably, but it certainly is not the substantial, if neglected, building that Heathcliff lives in.

Just as many buildings influenced Emily's great novel, so did many of the books she had read and loved. We have earlier mentioned James Hogg's *The Private Memoirs and Confessions of a Justified Sinner*. The hero, or should we say anti-hero, of the book is Robert Colwen, second son of the Laird of Dalcastle. He is determined to bring about the destruction of his elder brother George, and he does this through the help of a mysterious figure called Gil-Martin. The family feud at the heart of the book is familiar, but it is the dark undercurrent of the book that seeped into Emily's blood. Robert, who is surely less than sane, believes the form-changing Gil-Martin to be the Tsar of Russia and a man sent by God to show him the path of the righteous, but the reader soon recognises him as the Devil himself. Robert's last angry lament is very redolent of Fernando de Samara's speech in Emily's poem above, and it surely found an echo in Heathcliff's death too:

> Still am I living, though liker to a vision than a human being; but this is my last day of mortal existence ... Farewell, world, with all thy miseries; for comforts or enjoyments thou hast none! Farewell, woman, whom I have despised and shunned; whom, nevertheless, I desire to leave in charity! And thou, sun, bright emblem of a far brighter effulgence, I bid farewell to thee also! I do not now take my last look of thee, for to thy glorious orb a poor suicide's last earthly look be raised. But, ah! who is yon that I see approaching furiously – his stern face blackened with horrid despair! My hour is at hand.[7]

Another Scottish author even more loved by Emily was Sir Walter Scott, and we can clearly hear an echo of *The Bride of Lammermoor* in *Wuthering Heights*. In Scott's novel, the usurped hero is Edgar, whose Ravenswood Estate has been snatched by Sir William Ashton. Edgar falls in love with his enemy's daughter Lucy Ashton and they become engaged. Lucy's mother is the true villain of the piece in Scott's novel. Lady Ashton intercepts Edgar's letters while he is away in France, telling Lucy that Edgar has forgotten her, and arranges a marriage with the insipid Laird Bucklaw. Edgar returns on Lucy's wedding day, starting a dark chain of events that end the book. It is a novel full of high emotion and high drama, and it climaxes with Lucy stabbing Bucklaw on her wedding night, followed by her insanity and death, and finally the death of Edgar himself. It is clear that it is not just the name Edgar that Emily has taken, but the theme of a doomed love triangle, where misunderstandings lead only to death.

The Bride of Lammermoor is still read today, but the same cannot be said of a similarly titled novella that also influenced *Wuthering Heights* called *The Bridegroom of Barna*.[8] Written anonymously, it featured in the November 1840 edition of *Blackwood's Magazine*, so loved by the Brontës. Set in Tipperary, it tells the story of ill-fated lovers. Golden-haired Ellen Nugent and dark, brooding Hugh Lawlor are from rival families, and marry against the wishes of their parents. The wedding feast is on a wild, stormy night, during which the bridegroom is betrayed as a murderer by a one-armed scoundrel called Tom Bush. Lawlor escapes to the mountains, but Ellen dies of grief. In a precursor to Heathcliff's actions, Lawlor digs up his beloved's body and cradles her in his arms:

> By the side of Ellen Nugent's new-made grave sat the murderer Lawlor, enclosing in his arms the form that had once comprised all earth's love and beauty for him, and which, like a miser, with wild and maniac affection, he had unburied once more to clasp and contemplate.[9]

One person who we can say with surety did not influence the writing of *Wuthering Heights*, although his character may have been represented at least in part by both Heathcliff and Edgar, is Emily's brother Branwell. It is a calumny that some people still believe he was the true author, or at least co-author, of the novel – something first hinted at by Branwell's friend and biographer Francis Leyland. This lie was popular within some Victorian circles simply because they could not believe that a parson's daughter could have written such a wild, magical work. Knowing her and her influences as we do today, we can say for certain that she did. Branwell could turn out readable poems from time to time, but he never had it in him to write a *Wuthering Heights*, as summed up succinctly by Kaye Sugden in his 1929 biography of the Brontë family:

> [Leyland's biography of Branwell] attempts to maintain that his achievements as an author were such that he might easily have written all, or at least a part, of *Wuthering Heights*. We know, of course, for a fact that he did nothing of the sort; but even if we did not, the productions which Mr. Leyland prints in wearisome profusion are almost without exception so mediocre that we are quite convinced of his incapability … He was no genius, and all his sisters' fame will never make him one.[10]

The true author of the masterpiece that is *Wuthering Heights* took many influences, blended them with her own supremely powerful imagination, and created something far greater than the sum of its parts. Like Shakespeare before her, she takes source material and spins it into pure gold. There is only one person who had the internal fire, power and untamed brilliance to write *Wuthering Heights*: Emily Brontë.

UNREGARDING EYES

Why ask to know what date, what clime?
There dwelt our own humanity,
Power-worshippers from earliest time,
Foot-kissers of triumphant crime,
Crushers of helpless misery.
Crushing down Justice, honouring Wrong:
If that be feeble, this be strong.
Shedders of blood, shedders of tears:
Self-cursers avid of distress,
Yet mocking heaven with senseless prayers,
For mercy on the merciless.
It was the autumn of the year,
When grain grows yellow in the ear,
Day after day, from noon to noon,
The August sun blazed bright as June.
But we with unregarding eyes,
Saw panting earth and glowing skies,
No hand the reaper's sickle held,
Nor bound the ripe sheaves in the field.
Our corn was garnered months before,
Threshed out and kneaded-up with gore,

Ground when the ears were milky sweet,
With furious toil of hoofs and feet,
I, doubly cursed on foreign sod,
Fought neither for my home nor God.

('Why Ask to Know What Date, What Clime?', dated 13 May
1848)

THIS POEM COULD never be called one of Emily
Brontë's greatest, made up of confusing, apocalyptic
verse in an unspecified Gondal setting. It is also
incomplete and a reworking of a much longer poem
that itself lay unfinished from two years earlier, 'Why Ask
to Know the Date – the Clime?'[1] Despite this, it is a poem of
great significance and deserving of its place here, for these
twenty-five lines are the last words ever written by Emily
Brontë, the only poem she wrote after the publication of
Wuthering Heights, and the only words she composed in the
year of her death.

Wuthering Heights shows, without doubt, that Emily was
at the peak of her creative powers, as does her acclaimed
poem 'No Coward Soul is Mine', composed around the same
time. But the poem above is all Emily submitted to paper
in the two years that followed. Emily was a very proficient
writer of poetry, and she had found happiness and fulfilment
from writing since the days of her childhood, so just what
was it that made her stop so suddenly, and would she ever
have returned to her writing desk if consumption had not
abruptly claimed her? This is one of the great mysteries of
literature, but I believe the answer lies in both the aftermath
of the publication of her novel, and the tensions that were
growing within her parsonage home.

There is no doubt that Emily was furious at the time her
hidden book of poetry was unearthed, and was extremely
reticent to put her verse before the public. After the initial
explosion, she may have internalised her feelings on the
matter, characteristically for her, but they would still bubble to
the surface from time to time, leading to a strained quietness
so unlike the lively atmosphere that usually prevailed when
the sisters were together. We have a direct allusion to this in a
poem by Anne Brontë:

Why should such gloomy silence reign;
And why is all the house so drear,
When neither danger, sickness, pain,
Nor death, nor want have entered here?
We are as many as we were,
That other night, when all were gay,
And full of hope, and free from care;
Yet, is there something gone away.
The moon without as pure and calm,
Is shining as that night she shone;
but now, to us she brings no balm,
For something from our hearts is gone.
Something whose absence leaves a void,
A cheerless want in every heart.
Each feels the bliss of all destroyed,
And mourns the change – but each apart.
The fire is burning in the grate,
As redly as it used to burn,
But still the hearth is desolate,
Till Mirth and Love with Peace return.[2]

Anne's poem has two titles, both very revealing. When preparing it for a posthumous publication in 1850, Charlotte ironically titled it *Domestic Peace*, even though it obviously relates to a time when the silence in the house was far from peaceful. Anne herself gave it the title *Monday Night May 11th 1846*, so we can pinpoint exactly when it was written. The date was obviously significant, as no other Brontë poems are given a title of this nature. This was the month in which *Poems by Currer, Ellis and Acton Bell* was published, and it seems clear that this had reignited the argument between Emily and Charlotte. Emily had looked down upon the poems that contained her very essence, and saw that what once was written in ink by her own hand and safely hidden away was now printed on paper and available for the world to see – and judge. This was almost unbearable for Emily, especially when the people judging the work failed to understand it, or her.

Elizabeth Gaskell, in her famous biography of Charlotte Brontë, was keen to point out a subtle yet important difference between Emily and Anne:

> Emily was ... extremely reserved in manner. I distinguish reserve from shyness, because I imagine shyness would please, if it knew how; whereas, reserve is indifferent whether it pleases or not. Anne, like her eldest sister, was shy; Emily was reserved.[3]

I think Gaskell is wrong to make this distinction. Her observations on Emily are second-hand, snatched from conversations with Charlotte or gleaned from her interviews with Haworth villagers, who themselves had little knowledge of Emily. We get a different impression from a woman who came to know her as well as anyone outside the Brontë family, Ellen Nussey: 'She could be really vivacious in conversation, taking pleasure in giving pleasure.'[4]

Emily, then, was like Anne in this, as in so many things; she wanted to make people happy but was often misunderstood because of her extreme shyness. She typically projected an unconcerned exterior, as if treating sorrows and joys the same, but at heart she was very sensitive and an unkind word would always be remembered. This was another reason she had been so reticent about seeking a publisher, she was terrified of receiving bad reviews.

Emily had nothing to worry about when it came to *Poems by Currer, Ellis and Acton Bell*. It was little noticed and little reviewed, yet those who did review it were particularly positive about Emily's contributions, as in this review in *The Athenaeum*:

> A fine quaint spirit has the latter [Ellis Bell], which may have things to speak that men will be glad to hear – and an evident power of wing that may reach heights not yet attempted ...

How musical he can be, and how lightly and easily the music falls from his heart and pen.[5]

Both the lack of recognition from the book-buying public and the munificent reviews heartened Emily, allowing her to complete *Wuthering Heights* at a rapid pace, and alleviating any fears she may have had about entering the publishing deal with Thomas Cautley Newby. Once the contract was signed, however, the publisher seemed strangely reluctant to place the books before the public. Although Emily and Anne unhesitatingly agreed to the contract, miserly as it was, offered by Newby in July 1847, the books, with *Wuthering Heights* taking the first two volumes and *Agnes Grey* the third, were not released until the close of the year. It was frustrating to the sisters, but a smart commercial decision as, by this time, Charlotte had completed her second novel and it fared slightly better than *The Professor*. It was of course *Jane Eyre*, and Currer Bell became an overnight sensation when it was published in October 1847. This prompted Newby to finally unleash the books he held by the two other Bell brothers, in the hope of riding on its coat tails.

This arrangement was not to Emily's liking. Rather than being judged on its own merits, her novel was being compared to *Jane Eyre*, as if the Bells were just a single entity. This time, her work was much more widely reviewed, and as she read the notices her worst fears were realised: she had been wildly misunderstood, and the true greatness of her book was overlooked. One particularly unperceptive review came from *The Atlas*:

> *Wuthering Heights* is a strange, inartistic story ... The general effect is inexpressibly painful ... There is not in the entire dramatis personae a single character which is not utterly hateful or thoroughly contemptible. If you do not detest the person, you despise him; and if you do not despise him, you detest him with all your heart.[6]

The anonymous reviewer is being unfair, not only on Emily, or Ellis as he presumed, but on beneficent characters such as Nellie Dean and Zillah, and even Lockwood. They had failed to see the art in the book, but even they could not fail to be jolted by its power, as the final line of the review shows: 'The work of Currer Bell is a great performance; that of Ellis Bell is only a promise, but it is a colossal one.'[7]

The Examiner's reviewer found fault with the coarse language used in *Wuthering Heights*:

> It may be well also to be sparing of certain oaths and phrases, which do not materially contribute to any character ... It is the province of an artist to modify and in some cases refine what he beholds in the ordinary world. There never was a man whose daily life (that is to say, all his deeds and sayings, entire and without exception) constituted fit materials for a book of fiction.[8]

Emily Brontë was not a writer who could forget criticism. The above reviews were among five cuttings found, well thumbed, in her writing desk after her death.[9] Emily returned to them time and time again, reading the charges arrayed against her. While all the reviews found at least something positive to say about the book itself, it was the condemnation that lingered.

Later in the year, reviews began to appear from the United States of America, and again they lacked perception and attacked the Bell brothers and their coarse creations. By this time, Emily was beyond caring, almost beyond this world, as a sad letter from Charlotte revealed after she read E.P. Whipple's review in *The North American Review* to her fading sisters:

> What a bad set the Bells must be! What appalling books they write! Today as Emily appeared a little easier, I thought the Review would amuse her so I read it aloud to her and Anne. As I sat between them at our quiet but now somewhat melancholy fireside, I studied the two ferocious authors. Ellis, 'the man of

uncommon talents, but dogged, brutal, and morose', sat leaning back in his easy chair drawing his impeded breath as best he could, and looking, alas! piteously pale and wasted; it is not his wont to laugh, but he smiled half-amused and half in scorn as he listened. Acton was sewing, no emotion ever stirs him to loquacity, so he only smiled too, dropping at the same time a single word of calm amazement to hear his character so darkly portrayed. I wonder what the reviewer would have thought of his own sagacity could he have beheld the pair as I did.[10]

This, and earlier reviews from the British press, struck deep into Emily's heart – they were not merely attacking her, but her sisters too. Even worse, Charlotte herself misunderstood *Wuthering Heights*, as we can see from the preface she created for the 1850 reissue:

Her imagination, which was a spirit more sombre than sunny, more powerful than sportive, found in such traits material whence it wrought creations like Heathcliff, like Earnshaw, like Catherine. Having formed these beings, she did not know what she had done … Whether it is right or advisable to create things like Heathcliff, I do not know: I scarcely think it is.[11]

Charlotte, like many of the book's reviewers, was of the opinion that *Wuthering Heights* was too wild and untamed, but that the author would do better with her second novel. The question of a successor to Emily's sole novel continues to puzzle and intrigue us because of one tantalising letter from Thomas Cautley Newby to Ellis Bell:

I am much obliged by your kind note & shall have great pleasure in making arrangements for your next novel. I would not hurry its completion, for I think you are quite right not to let it go before the world until well satisfied with it, for much depends on your new work if it be an improvement on your first you will have established yourself as a first rate novelist, but if it falls short the Critics will be too apt to say that you have expended your talent in your first novel.[12]

It is a letter that divides opinion. Some believe that Newby meant the letter for Acton Bell and had addressed it incorrectly, as Anne was at that time preparing her second novel, *The Tenant of Wildfell Hall*, but it was found in Emily's writing desk so we can be confident it was intended for her. The great Brontë historian Juliet Barker conjectures from this letter that Emily had been working on a new novel for the last two years of her life, and this is why she produced no other work in that time, but in my opinion, that makes little sense. Cautley's letter is in response to 'a note'. We know from Emily's letters to Ellen that her epistles were typically brief affairs. We also know that Emily was a rapid writer, so would she really spend two years on a work of which we have not a word in existence today?

It seems to me there are two possibilities. One is that Newby sent an earlier letter to Emily, asking her for an update on a second novel that she had already agreed to (as we can surmise from Newby's publication of Anne's second book, despite his earlier shabby treatment of her). Emily sends a terse response saying she is taking her time with it (having not actually contemplated writing one), which, in turn, leads to Newby's letter above. Another possibility is that Emily, in an effort to raise her own spirits, had sent a letter to her publisher stating that she was thinking of writing another novel if he would be interested in taking it. In either scenario, it seems unlikely to me that she ever commenced any meaningful work on the book.

The poem 'Why Ask to Know What Date, What Clime?' is evidence of Emily's mind and creative powers in these last two years: all she could do was eviscerate an earlier poem, not add to it. The muse had left Emily, and perhaps the visions that drove her creativity had ceased to appear as well. She brooded on how writing had caused a rift between the sisters, and despaired at the reviews that attacked her and a work that, in many ways, was an extension of her inner self. The critics with unregarding eyes were shedders of blood while she, the mocked writer, is the shedder of tears.

In time, Emily might have regained her visionary zeal for writing, and might have returned with works of incredible beauty and power, but time was a commodity in short supply. Another reason that she put aside her paper is that real life, for the first time since childhood, had now become more important than Gondal and the imagination. In Anne's poem, which we saw earlier, we hear that 'neither danger, sickness, pain, nor death, nor want' have entered the parsonage. They were about to do exactly that.

18

THE SLAVE OF FALSEHOOD, PRIDE, AND PAIN

Well, some may hate, and some may scorn,
And some may quite forget thy name;
But my sad heart must ever mourn,
Thy ruined hopes, thy blighted fame!
'Twas thus I thought, an hour ago,
Even weeping o'er that wretches woe;
One word turned back my gushing tears,
And lit my altered eye with sneers.
Then 'Bless the friendly dust,' I said,
'That hides thy unlamented head!
Vain as thou wert, and weak as vain,
The slave of Falsehood, Pride, and Pain, –
My heart has nought akin to thine;
Thy soul is powerless over mine.'
But these were thoughts that vanished too;
Unwise, unholy, and untrue;
Do I despise the timid deer,
Because his limbs are fleet with fear?
Or, would I mock the wolf's death-howl,

Because his form is gaunt and foul?
Or, hear with joy the leveret's cry,
Because it cannot bravely die?
No! Then above his memory
Let Pity's heart as tender be;
Say, 'Earth, lie lightly on that breast,
And, kind Heaven, grant that spirit rest!'

('Stanzas To –', dated 14 November 1839)

THE ENIGMATIC TITLE of this poem keeps the reader guessing whom Emily Brontë is addressing the stanzas to, but it can be read as an indicator of Emily's conflicted feelings towards her only brother, Branwell. It may be a precursor of Emily's feelings after the death of Branwell, even though it was written nearly nine years before his untimely death aged just 31. Even by 1839, however, Branwell had begun a descent into addiction that would eventually destroy him, and Emily was a keen, if taciturn, observer of her siblings' behaviour. The year of this poem marked the end of Branwell's dream of becoming a portrait painter. In 1839, he gave up his studio in Bradford and returned home to Haworth, an uncertain future stretching ahead of him, one that was very different to the one he and Emily had imagined just a few years earlier.

Patrick Branwell was once the great hope for the Brontë family; the boy who would continue the name and blood line. Unfortunately, he would become better known to the world for his troubled life and his debilitating addictions rather than the talents he once possessed.

Emily Brontë was born just over a year after her brother, making them the closest of all the Brontë siblings in terms of age, but they were not close in character, as Emily suffered from shyness while Branwell suffered with pride. Young Branwell was made to feel he was the most important of the children; in a word, he was indulged, and he learned that he liked to be indulged.

From an early age, Branwell had a hatred of regimented discipline and often misbehaved, as we see from Emily's answer from behind the mask as a child.[1] These traits became more pronounced as he grew older, but it is important to recognise the reasons behind this. Branwell was 4½ when his mother died after a long and painful illness, not old enough to understand what was happening, yet old enough to comprehend a loss and to remember forever the struggles his mother had to endure. When he was 8, his two eldest sisters, Maria and Elizabeth, also died, and the loss of Maria especially was painful to him.

It was Maria who had bounced her little brother on her knee, reading to him and helping him learn his letters. She had knelt by him in the evening, teaching him prayers. As Branwell later remembered in his poem *Caroline*, in which the dead figure of Caroline represents his eldest sister, she was teaching him much more than that:

> She lay, as I had seen her lie
> On many a happy night before,
> When I was humbly kneeling by –
> Whom she was teaching to adore;
> Oh, just as when by her I prayed,
> And she to heaven sent up her prayer,
> She lay with flowers about her head –
> Though formal grave clothes hid her hair![2]

Aged just 8, three crushing blows had already been delivered to this physically slight yet mentally agile young boy, and he never recovered. It could be from the day of his sister Maria's death that his faith began to dissipate, until he eventually disavowed religion completely. Prayers seemed a mockery when the beloved sister who had taught them to him had been so cruelly and arbitrarily snatched away.

With both Marias gone, mother and sister, there was also less of a check on his impulses, and he increasingly acted first and thought later. As a youth, he was already demonstrating characteristics that were far from the norm. He could be fired with an unstoppable energy and enthusiasm, writing and drawing brilliantly with both hands at the same time, but at other times he was consumed with ennui and self-loathing, unable to concentrate his energies on one task for any length of time. In today's world, we might speculate that Branwell's early torments had led to him developing bipolar disorder, but of course that diagnosis, and the help that would come with it, was unavailable in the nineteenth century.

As Patrick's question to her masked self shows, it was Emily more than any of his siblings who challenged his more objectionable behaviour, even engaging in a physical tussle with her brother when he would not listen to her admonitions. Emily was always taller and stronger than her brother; in a fight she could easily beat him, or 'whip' him, as the Yorkshire parlance goes. It was an affront to his pride, but one he had to endure.

We have heard how the gifting of twelve toy soldiers to Branwell set the Brontës' creative talents in motion, and have read Charlotte's account of that momentous occasion. Branwell too, however, gave his version of this day, and it differs notably:

> I carried them [the soldiers] to Emily, Charlotte and Anne. They each took up a soldier, gave them names, which I consented to, and I gave Charlotte Twemy, to Emily Pare, to Anne Trot to take care of them, although they were to be mine and I to have the disposal of them as I would.[3]

Here we see Branwell placing himself in charge of the situation again, graciously allowing his sisters to have a soldier each, and consenting to their names. Also of note here is that Branwell mentions Emily first, rather than his oldest sister Charlotte, as if Emily's physical supremacy bears more weight with Branwell than her age. It is an indication that although there could be tensions between them, a close bond had also formed, a bond reflected in Emily's poem 'Stanzas To –', and borne out by her actions in adulthood.

Branwell took the initial lead in their childhood writings, acting as first 'editor' of their microscopic magazines, referring to himself within the writings as 'chief genius Brannii'.

When Charlotte was sent to Roe Head School in July 1831, however, he found himself sidelined. Emily wasted little time in establishing her own imaginary world of Gondal in alliance with Anne. Branwell was conspicuously missing from Gondal, his adventures of the imagination brought to a sudden end.

In October 1835, Emily returned to Haworth from her brief sojourn at Roe Head, to be replaced by Anne. It was around this time that Branwell returned to the parsonage from an unsuccessful attempt to make his way in the world. The exact dates are impossible to trace, as is the exact sequence of events, but the summer of 1835 saw plans made for Branwell to enter the Royal Academy of Arts in London to train as an artist.[4] All we know for sure is that Branwell never made it into the academy.

Many reasons have been postulated for this failure. It could be that Branwell simply could not raise the funds for an extended stay in London, or that having arrived at the academy he was overcome by one of his crushing attacks of self-doubt and fled back to Yorkshire. It has even been suggested that Branwell never actually ventured to London at all, and that his talk of doing so was his usual bluster. There is a testimony, however, from a man of Leeds called Woolven, who knew Branwell during his time on the railway. Woolven stated he had first met Branwell many years earlier in the Castle Tavern, in London's Holborn district, where he was regaling people with feats of memory and demonstrating an 'unusual flow of language and strength of memory'.[5] This seems entirely consistent with what we know of Branwell at this time, and it seems most probable that he did indeed make a trip to London in the autumn of 1835, but that his stay was very short lived.

In October 1835 then, Emily and Branwell found themselves the only siblings at home in Haworth. They had both experienced failures, but reacted to them in different ways. Emily was withdrawn, chastened by her inability to spend even a short period of time away from her home and the beloved moors around it. Branwell was boisterous once more, and determined to prove that his failure in London was but an aberration.

This initial, but not final, attempt at becoming an artist made him determined to succeed in another creative pursuit: writing. Branwell was a very keen poet, having already had verse published in Yorkshire newspapers under his Angrian pseudonym of Northangerland. He dreamt of writing for his favourite magazine, *Blackwood's*, and on 7 December 1837 he wrote the first of a series of letters to them, asking to be added to their staff. These letters did little to advance his cause, however, although they amused the magazine enough for them to hold on to them for posterity. Branwell's unworldliness is very apparent in them, as is his overblown sense of importance. He ended the letter:

> Now, sir, do not act like a commonplace person, but like a man willing to examine for himself. Do not turn from the naked truth of my letters, but prove me – and if I do not stand the proof, I will not further press myself upon you. If I do stand it, why, you have lost an able writer in James Hogg, and God grant you may gain one in Patrick Branwell Brontë.[6]

By this time, the characters of Emily and Branwell had become polarised: the brother desperate to see his name in print, the sister who would later be desperate to avoid her name appearing in print. This is the vanity that Emily talks of in her poem, a vanity that left Branwell 'the slave of falsehood, pride and pain'.

Emily and her sisters had held high hopes for their brother, and indeed were relying upon him to succeed. Their father was ageing and his eyesight failing; if the worst should happen and he was no longer able to practise as a priest, then Branwell would be expected to step up as the family's main breadwinner until his sisters could find careers or husbands and start households of their own.

Despite his Royal Academy debacle, Branwell still loved to paint, and in May 1838 he moved to Bradford, lodging with Mr and Mrs Kirby, and set up studio as a portrait painter. He revelled in the new artistic circles in which he moved, with the young and celebrated sculptor Joseph Bentley Leyland becoming a close friend. Many of Branwell's portraits from this time are now in the collection of the Brontë Parsonage Museum, and they are perfectly competent pieces, even if lacking in brilliance, often depicting local men and women staring boldly out of the canvas with a dark and stormy background behind them.

Given time, and further practice mixed with experience, there is every chance that he could have become a portrait artist of some note, if not fortune. As is so often the case, however, time was not on his side. These were the very early days of photography, so the middle and upper classes still turned to artists to have their likenesses captured, but that made competition fierce, with a multitude of artists plying their trade. Branwell was finding it hard to gain commissions and running up debts, and his regular drinking sprees in establishments like Bradford's Midland Hotel did little to help.

By October 1839, Branwell had given up his artistic ambitions and returned to Haworth, but this time failure had deflated him. He looked at the horizon, the years stretching out ahead of him, and wondered how he could fill them. In his heart, he considered himself a genius, but there now seemed little hope of the wider world recognising his talents. He was sentenced to a life of mediocrity, and from his arrival back in Haworth he sought solace in a numbing new friend – opium.

Opium was widely available in the late 1830s, and it could even be found in cough medicines and easily obtained treatments for complaints such as dental pain. Looking back from today, however, we can fall into the misconception of thinking this meant that taking opium, or laudanum, as it was called when mixed in a tincture with alcohol, was acceptable at the time. In fact, it was considered a lowly pursuit, often turned to by the poorest and most desperate members of society as it offered them oblivion for less than the price of a drink of spirits.

Even in 1839 the effects of opium addiction were well known, and widely eschewed by the sections of society who thought of themselves as respectable. For Branwell, however, it offered him the soaring highs that he could not find in reality, that he had seemingly no hope of finding. Opium addiction clouded the remaining years of his life, although he did manage to wean himself off the drug temporarily at one point. It was opium, even more than the alcohol that he also became addicted to, that later resulted in his uncontrollable rages and his threats against his family and himself.

This is the 'one word' in Emily's poem that turns back her gushing tears and replaces them with a sneer. When feeling most sorry for what Branwell has become, she remembers that single word, opium, and her pity turns to revulsion and anger. By November 1839, when the poem was composed, she had already seen how the drug affected him, and she had enough knowledge of her brother's addictive personality to guess where it would lead.

Opium was a hateful substance to Emily, but had she tried it herself, perhaps urged on by her brother or in the form of a medicine given to her – possibly after her return from Roe Head School, when her life was felt to be in danger? Certainly, there is one particular passage in *Wuthering Heights* that reeks of the opium poppy. The narrator, Lockwood, is trapped at Wuthering Heights by a storm. Falling asleep, he dreams that he is in attendance at a monstrous sermon held by the raging preacher Jabes Branderham. This sermon is divided into 490 parts, each as long as a sermon in itself, and all experienced with perfect clarity during his dream[7] – a dream of minutes that encapsulated an address of more than two days in duration.

This is reminiscent of the terrors that some opium addicts experience. In his seminal autobiographical work of 1821,

Confessions of an English Opium-Eater, Thomas de Quincey names it as the very worst pain of opium, so that he dreaded going to sleep:

> The sense of space, and in the end, the sense of time, were both powerfully affected ... Space swelled, and was amplified to an extent of unutterable infinity ... I sometimes seemed to have lived for 70 or 100 years in one night; nay; sometimes had feelings representative of a millennium passed in that time, or, however, of a duration far beyond the limits of any human experience.[8]

Is Lockwood then an opium taker himself, and could that also explain the vision that follows of Cathy clawing at his window? Even more pertinently, had Emily Brontë herself some experience of the night terrors that opium can bring? It seems more likely that Emily had knowledge of such things through watching the sufferings of her brother, and through her own knowledge of de Quincey's work. De Quincey was, after all, one of the writers to whom Emily, Charlotte and Anne sent a copy of *Poems by Currer, Ellis and Acton Bell* in June 1847.

Branwell's behaviour grew worse with advancing years, and yet Emily still clung to the familial bonds between them. Branwell the man was also the same boy who had written her childhood imaginings down in his little books, and who had supplemented her piano lessons with lessons of his own until the pupil far outreached the teacher. He had led her on her earliest excursions to the moors, those walks that would become the defining moments of her life.

This is the revelation that informs the second half of Emily's poem: Branwell was becoming a wreck of a man, but although others may turn their back on him, she never would. She would protect him and forgive him, even if she did have to whip him verbally first. As the years passed by, she would have more and more opportunities to do so.

Branwell suffered two further mortal blows. In 1840, he found a job as a senior clerk on the railways that paid well and offered good prospects for the future. Branwell neglected his duties, however, and spent his time writing, sketching and drinking in the inns of Halifax and Luddendenfoot. It was found that a clerk supposedly under his supervision had been stealing from the railway, and in March 1842 Branwell was summarily dismissed.

An even more disastrous position was procured for him in January 1843. Anne Brontë was at that time a highly valued governess to the wealthy Robinson family of Thorp Green Hall, near York. When they talked of taking on a male tutor for their son Edmund, Anne had no hesitation in suggesting her brother for the role. He would stay there until July 1845, but he took more of an interest in the mistress of the house than her son. Lydia Robinson was in her mid-forties, but still considered an attractive woman, and it seems that she took a shine to the new tutor: he was vivacious, a quick talker and a quicker thinker, and a contrast to her ageing, often angry and choleric, husband.

To what extent an affair between Branwell and Lydia progressed can only be conjecture, but there seems little doubt that an affair of some kind did take place and that this led to his dismissal. Back in Haworth, Branwell turned again to opium and drank more heavily than ever before, whenever he could afford it. The depression he had sunk into was made far worse by the events following on from the death of Edmund Robinson in May 1846. Branwell, as unworldly as ever, firmly believed that Lydia Robinson would marry him, not considering that he was a penniless and dissolute man way below her social position.

Marriage, of course, was out of the question, and she sent a letter to Branwell telling him that her husband's will had stipulated that they could never see each other again.[9] It was a falsehood, but Branwell believed it and it sent him into an even more pronounced decline.

The inns adjacent to the parsonage, the Black Bull, the King's Arms and the White Lion, now saw another Branwell. Gone was the bonhomie that had seen him called for to entertain coach parties when they arrived, and in its place was an all-encompassing bitterness and a desire for the release of death. By 1847 he was suffering from the effects of delirium tremens, sometimes collapsing on inn floors in a fit. At other times, his friend and the Haworth sexton, John Brown, would have to drag him back to the parsonage. If Brown was away on duty, it is easy to imagine Emily being seconded to this role, possessing as she did the physical strength to carry and drag him.

This strength was to prove particularly useful one night. Branwell had lost the patience to read, but had taken a magazine to bed to look at the pictures by candlelight. In a stupor, he fell asleep and, looking in at his room as she often did, Anne found that he was lying in bed with the sheets around him on fire. Anne was unable to move his sleeping dead weight so, running downstairs, she whispered in Emily's ear. Emily had no trouble in hauling Branwell out of his bed, and the two girls then put the fire out using pitchers of water. This scene is reminiscent of *Jane Eyre*, but with Branwell playing the role of both Bertha and Rochester.

Increasingly, it was the Bertha side of Branwell's character that was taking charge. He would shriek and moan all night long, keeping his family awake, or else he would threaten that in the morning either he or his father, who now insisted on sleeping with him for his safety, would be dead.

In the face of such provocation, Charlotte, who had been the close companion of her brother in childhood, broke off all communications with him for the final two years of his life. Emily, however, would not abandon him. She waited by the parsonage door, helping her drunken brother to walk the stairs to his bedroom, or carrying him there when he was incapable.

By September 1848 there had been an irrevocable change in her brother. He had become gaunt and foul, just like the wolf in Emily's poem, and his own death-howl was close at hand. Branwell's friend, Francis Grundy, after a visit to Haworth, paints a horrific scene of the dissipated and half-mad Branwell, with his lips endlessly shaking.[10] Looking back at him for the last time, Grundy found him doubled over in the middle of the street, crying. We also hear that he was so weak that he could not lift his leg up one solitary step, and William Brown, brother of the sexton John, had to help him. It is also telling that the person to whom the poem at the head of this chapter is addressed is compared to a dying leveret, a young hare, a symbol of weakness that Emily would later use in *Wuthering Heights*, when Cathy berates Edgar, 'your type is not a lamb, it's a sucking leveret!'[11]

By 22 September, Branwell was confined to his bed with Emily taking on the role of chief nursemaid. Gone now was the anger, and at last he was at peace with the world. His final moments came on Sunday 24 September 1848. John Brown was by his bedside and was about to leave it to ring the bells summoning people to church. Branwell suddenly called out, 'John, I'm dying!'[12] Patrick, Emily, Anne and Charlotte were called to his room. Patrick prayed fervently, and Branwell at last whispered a word that had not escaped his lips for a decade, 'amen'. With a herculean effort, he rose from the bed, embraced his father, and died.

Emily's poem of 1839 had looked forward to that day, nine years later. Now in life, as on paper, she could say, 'Earth, lie lightly on that breast and, kind heaven, grant that spirit rest!' It was Emily who had cared for Branwell during his final days, and who had carried him, literally and emotionally, during the preceding weeks. She was soon to find that she would have to pay the ultimate price for her filial love and charity.

19

COURAGE TO ENDURE

Riches I hold in light esteem;
And Love I laugh to scorn;
And lust of fame was but a dream,
That vanished with the morn:
And if I pray, the only prayer,
That moves my lips for me,
Is, 'Leave the heart that now I bear,
And give me liberty!'
Yes, as my swift days near their goal,
'Tis all that I implore;
In life and death, a chainless soul,
With courage to endure.

('The Old Stoic', dated 1 March 1841)

B RANWELL'S LIFESTYLE ENSURED that he was never likely to survive into old age, and yet he had been relatively healthy when not suffering the effects of delirium tremens. Indeed, in the year before his death he had complained to a friend that he would live too long:

> I know … my father cannot have long to live, and that when he dies my evening, which is already twilight, will become night – that I shall have then a constitution still so strong that it will keep me years in torture and despair when I should every hour pray that I might die.[1]

Branwell's demise came suddenly, but when it came it was not because of alcohol or opium, but consumption – what we know today as tuberculosis. In 1972, the eminent British physician Professor Philip Rhodes appraised the health and deaths of the Brontës based upon recorded facts. His conclusion on Branwell was, 'Probably as a result of his carousing and drug-taking, and even the possibility of cirrhosis of the liver, his resistance to tuberculosis would be weakened and this finally killed him.'[2]

This explains Branwell's rapid decline, but where did tuberculosis come from? Haworth was a sickly, infested village, with death rates as high as the worst slums of London and where over 41 per cent of the population died before the age of 6,[3] but by far the biggest killers were typhus and cholera. Tuberculosis was an infection carried from person to person, a killer of the crowded cities, and relatively rare in Haworth – so it is more than an anomaly that five of the six Brontë children should die of it.

The sad truth is that one day in July 1848 not only changed the course of literature forever, it also led directly to the death of Branwell Brontë and then to the deaths of Emily Brontë and Anne Brontë, like dominoes falling long after the first domino has been pushed. The day referred to is 7 July 1848. On that day, a letter arrived at Haworth Parsonage that sent both Charlotte and Anne into a frenzy. It was from Charlotte's publisher, George Smith. He had heard from an American contact that Thomas Cautley Newby, publisher of *Wuthering Heights* and *Agnes Grey*, had been telling people that all the Bell brothers were one person using three different names. It was an accusation of dishonesty that could not go unanswered, but Emily's reaction reveals much of how she was feeling at this time.

A letter back would be no proof at all, so the only way to clear their name was to go to London in person, meet George Smith and finally reveal the truth. Charlotte and Anne acted straight away, and that very evening they were on a train from Leeds to London, retracing the journey Emily had made en route to Brussels six and a half years previously. Emily, however, had no desire to go. Consenting to the publication of her work had been enough of a blow; she could not consent to abandon the mask of Ellis Bell that still afforded her some protection. It is a sign of Emily's disillusionment with writing at this time to rank alongside her two-year absence from work.

To both Charlotte and Anne honour was everything – they simply had to journey to London to answer Smith's letter. Once at the office, they astonished the dashing young publisher by revealing that the brothers Currer and Acton Bell were in fact the curate's daughters, Charlotte and Anne Brontë. The Brontë sisters were at last before the world, but Emily had forced them to make a solemn promise that her identity would remain secret. The promise was broken, as we can see from a plea that Charlotte sent to W.S. Williams, whom she had met in London, at the end of July:

Permit me to caution you not to speak of sisters when you write to me. I mean, do not use the word in plural. 'Ellis Bell' will not endure to be alluded to under any other appellation than the 'nom de plume'. I committed a grand error in betraying his identity to you and Mr. Smith. It was inadvertent – the words 'we are three sisters' escaped me before I was aware. I regretted the avowal the moment I had made it; I regret it bitterly now, for I find it is against every feeling and intention of Ellis Bell.[4]

This letter shows that Emily was still furious at the revelation of Charlotte's indiscretion, twenty days after her return with Anne from London, but this unexpected news was far from the worst thing that the sisters brought back with them. Cold weather and a cruel east wind at the start of the year had left all the sisters with persistent coughs, and some have speculated that this could be a sign of tuberculosis. Coughs were far from uncommon in the cold environs of Haworth Parsonage, however, and although a severe cold or influenza may have weakened the immune systems of the Brontë children it was not a forewarning of consumption. For the source of the tuberculosis that laid Emily under the flagstones of St Michael and All Angels Church, we turn again to the diagnosis of Professor Philip Rhodes:

She [Emily] might have collected an overwhelming dose of tubercle bacilli from Branwell. She seems to have been the practical one about the household and may well have been Branwell's nurse and so liable to massive infection ... It is of especial interest that Charlotte and Anne made a hurried journey to London in July, 1848 ... Could one or other of the sisters have picked up a further dose of tubercle bacilli which when they returned to Haworth they handed on to Branwell and to Emily? This seems a most likely supposition. Almost certainly one or other of them introduced a new pathogenic element into the closed community of Haworth Parsonage, which wreaked so much havoc so quickly.[5]

The sad truth is that either Charlotte or Anne contracted tuberculosis while in the crowded streets of London, where the disease was endemic. Unwittingly introduced to Haworth Parsonage, its first victim was Branwell, who was particularly susceptible because of his disparate lifestyle; Emily's pity for her brother, leading her to carry him upstairs and nurse him, ensured that she too caught a fatal dose, and Anne followed suit. The argument between Charlotte and Emily over the revelation of her real name, a moment when she seemed full of health and vigour as well as indignation, came when she had just five months left to live.

Branwell was buried in the Brontë family vault beneath Haworth's church on 28 September 1848, but the funeral service, as was customary, was held later, on the first day of October. It was conducted by William Morgan, the man who had christened him thirty-one years earlier. It was at this service that Emily became racked by a cough; it was an ominous sign. Making the short walk back to the parsonage, she would doubtless have looked to her left and seen the moors stretching away into the distance, the moors over which her pitiable brother had guided her in their infancy. Another coughing fit took hold; it was time to go indoors. The moors would be there for eternity, always bleak yet always majestic, but Emily Brontë would never walk upon them again.

The rapid progress of Emily's illness was summed up by Charlotte in her biographical notice of her sister:

> Never in all her life had she lingered over any task that lay before her, and she did not linger now. She sank rapidly, she made haste to leave us. Yet, while physically she perished, mentally she grew stronger than we had yet known her. Day by day, when I saw with what a front she met suffering, I looked on her with an anguish of wonder and love. I have never seen anything like it.[6]

The mental anguish of Emily's family is also evident in a series of letters from Charlotte to Ellen Nussey and W.S. Williams. An initial concern was conveyed to Ellen on 29 October:

> I feel much more uneasy about my sisters than myself just now.
> Emily's cold and cough are very obstinate; I fear she has pain in
> the chest – and I sometimes catch a shortness in her breathing
> when she has moved at all quickly – she looks very, very thin
> and pale. Her reserved nature occasions one great uneasiness of
> mind. It is useless to question her – you get no answers – it is still
> more useless to recommend remedies – they are never adopted.[7]

The fear is obvious; shortness of breath and chest pains are
associated with the consumption that killed Branwell, and two
decades earlier had snatched away Maria and Elizabeth. Emily
was hiding her symptoms, but already, less than a month since her
coughing fit at her brother's memorial service, she was becoming
emaciated. Five days after her letter to Ellen, Charlotte's fears
were growing, as she revealed to W.S. Williams, the man who
had first discerned the brilliance of *Jane Eyre* and who had now
become one of his author's chief comforters:

> I would fain hope that Emily is a little better this evening, but
> it is difficult to ascertain this: she is a real stoic in illness, she
> neither seeks nor will accept sympathy; to put any question, to
> offer any aid is to annoy; she will not yield a step before pain or
> sickness till forced; not one of her ordinary avocations will she
> voluntary renounce: you must look on, and see her do what she
> is unfit to do, and not dare to say a word; a painful necessity for
> those to whom her life, health and existence are as precious as
> the life in their veins.[8]

This was a time of torment and frustration for Emily; she
could no longer do what she had become accustomed to do. She
could no longer take her long strides across the moors to the
meeting of the waters. She bore the great physical discomfort
with a steely determination, but her family now suffered
mental tortures that were harder to bear. To Anne, she was the
beloved twin-like sister, to Charlotte the worshipped genius,

stronger than a man, and to her father she was the apple of his eye and his right hand, but now all three had to watch Emily fade before their eyes without daring to raise a word.

Charlotte's publishers showed their true worth at this time, as they did again months later during Anne's final illness. George Smith sent Charlotte the sum of £100 against the early sales of *Jane Eyre*, and he also sent a large collection of books for Emily to read. W.S. Williams offered assistance of another kind. He was a firm believer in the efficacy of homoeopathic medicine and sent a letter urging Emily to try it, but the suggestion was dismissed, as a disconsolate Charlotte reported:

> I put your most friendly letter into Emily's hands as soon as I had myself perused it, taking care however not to say a word in favour of homoeopathy, that would not have answered; it is best usually to leave her to form her own judgement and <u>especially</u> not to advocate the side you wish her to favour; if you do she is sure to lean in the opposite direction, and ten to one will argue herself into non-compliance. Hitherto she has refused medicine, rejected medical advice – no reasoning, no entreaty has availed to induce her to see a physician; after reading your letter she said 'Mr Williams' intention was kind and good, but he was under a delusion – Homoeopathy was only another form of Quackery'.[9]

Even though homoeopathy still has many supporters today, the considered opinion of most medical professionals is that Emily's pronouncement on it was correct. It is also true that the conventional medicine available at that time was unlikely to be of any assistance, but we should remember that Emily had no way of knowing that: people in the first half of the nineteenth century had as much faith in the likes of 'Godbold's Vegetable Balsam' as we have in the latest medicines of our modern world. Godbold's advertised itself as a 'life saving elixir' and 'an infallible remedy for consumptions, asthma and coughs', but Emily would not touch it.

A day after her letter to Williams, Charlotte sent another letter to Ellen and by now there was no disguising the seriousness of Emily's condition:

I told you Emily was ill in my last letter – she has not rallied yet – she is <u>very</u> ill: I believe if you were to see her your impression would be that there is no hope: a more hollow, wasted pallid aspect I have not yet beheld. The deep tight cough continues; the breathing after the least exertion is a rapid pant – and these symptoms are accompanied by pain in the chest and side ... In this state, she resolutely refuses to see a doctor; she will give no explanation of her feelings, she will scarcely allow her illness to be alluded to. Our position is, and has been for some weeks, exquisitely painful. God only knows how all this is to terminate ... I think Emily seems the nearest thing to my heart in this world.[10]

By the start of December, Emily's illness was reaching its termination, and yet she still would not see a doctor. In desperation, Charlotte wrote to a specialist in the treatment of consumption, Dr Epps, as recommended by her publishers Smith and Williams. Her letter to Epps is a lengthy, revealing and moving account of the full horror of Emily's daily existence at this time:

A peculiar reserve of character renders it difficult to draw from her all the symptoms of her malady, but as far as they can be ascertained they are as follows ... Her appetite failed; she evinced a continual thirst with a craving for acids and required a constant change of beverage ... In appearance she grew rapidly emaciated, her pulse – the only time she allowed it to be felt – was found to be 115 per minute ... Expectoration accompanies the cough. The shortness of breath is aggravated by the slightest exertion. The patient's sleep is supposed to be tolerably good at intervals but disturbed by paroxysms of coughing. Her resolution to contend against illness being very fixed she has never consented to lie in bed for a single day – she sits up from 7 in the morning till 10 at night. All medical aid she has rejected – insisting that Nature shall be left to take her own course.[11]

The medicine recommended by Epps was, of course, rejected as all the other suggestions had been, and so the question has to be asked why Emily refused help at the time she needed it most, when it could not have done her any more harm, and when doing so would have brought comfort to her family?

One Emily Brontë expert conjectured that, being used to robust health, she might not even have realised how ill she was,[12] but surely previous good health would have made her current illness even more noticeable to her? Emily's symptoms were so severe, and her appearance so wasted, that there could be no doubt that she was closing in on death, and her actions, or rather her lack of actions, show she had accepted that. She had become like the old stoic in her poem of 1841: in the face of pain and suffering she would not despair, she would endure.

Emily believed that her death, imminent as it was, would liberate her from bodily suffering and free her chainless, endless soul that was the same in life and in death. She was taking solace in her beliefs, and the last line quoted above from Charlotte's statement to Dr Epps is very telling – Emily insisted that nature be left to take her own course. Nature was everything to Emily, and she saw herself as part of the natural cycle just as much as the plants that grow steadily, reach full bloom and then seem to wither and die, only to flourish again when the warming spring returns. Death was a part of the life cycle, inevitable from the moment of birth, but death was not the end in Emily's eyes, it was a new beginning.

One of the tasks Emily insisted upon carrying out, despite becoming weaker by the day, was feeding the dogs she loved so much: Anne's Flossy and her own Keeper. On the evening of 18 December, she took them a handful of meat and bread crumbs, but a gust of wind blowing under the door left her staggering in pain and in danger of falling to the floor.[13] Anne and Charlotte, who were keeping watch on her every movement now, went to help her, but a stern look stopped them in their tracks; Emily composed herself and fed the dogs as if nothing had happened, but it was to be the final meal she would deliver.

The next day, 19 December, she rose again and insisted on dressing herself and descending the stairs, but her movements were still more laboured and painful. She may have been blind by this time, as she had failed to recognise a sprig of moorland heather that Charlotte had gathered for her earlier in the month. One of the household, presumably Anne, tried to help her comb her long hair, but the comb slipped from her grasp and onto the fire – it remains in the Brontë Parsonage Museum today, with its middle section burnt away.

By noon, it was obvious that the final change had come. At last, Emily made the concession that her sisters and father had prayed for, saying, 'If you send for a doctor, I will see him now.'[14] Emily did not die suddenly, like Branwell, or calmly, as Anne was to do six months later. Her final hours were a struggle that was terrible to behold, yet through all her ordeal she had the courage to endure. Tradition dictates that she died on the sofa in the parsonage living room. Some dispute this, and point to Charlotte's comment that Keeper 'lay at the side of her dying-bed' in a letter to W.S. Williams in June 1849, but the sofa itself could have played the role of this bed, with the dying Emily stretched upon it and Charlotte and Anne holding her hands as her life was ripped away, her father praying and weeping nearby.

At two o'clock on 19 December 1848, Emily Jane Brontë died aged 30. Nature had completed its cycle, and she had 'died in the arms of those who loved her'.[15] The life of Emily Brontë, parson's daughter of Haworth, was at an end, but the life and legend of Emily Brontë, the writer of genius, was just beginning.

20

A FURTHER SHORE

'O day! he cannot die,
When thou so fair art shining!
O Sun, in such a glorious sky,
So tranquilly declining;
He cannot leave thee now,
While fresh west winds are blowing,
And all around his youthful brow,
Thy cheerful light is glowing!
Edward, awake, awake –
The golden evening gleams,
Warm and bright on Arden's lake –
Arouse thee from thy dreams!
Beside thee, on my knee,
My dearest friend, I pray,
That thou, to cross the eternal sea,
Wouldst yet one hour delay:
I hear its billows roar –
I see them foaming high;
But no glimpse of a further shore,
Has blest my straining eye.
Believe not what they urge,

Of Eden isles beyond;
Turn back, from that tempestuous surge,
To thy own native land.
It is not death, but pain,
That struggles in thy breast –
Nay, rally, Edward, rouse again;
I cannot let thee rest!'
One long look, that sore reproved me,
For the woe I could not bear –
One mute look of suffering moved me,
To repent my useless prayer:
And, with sudden check, the heaving,
Of distraction passed away;
Not a sign of further grieving,
Stirred my soul that awful day.
Paled, at length, the sweet sun setting;
Sunk to peace the twilight breeze:
Summer dews fell softly, wetting,
Glen, and glade, and silent trees.
Then his eyes began to weary,
Weighed beneath a mortal sleep;
And their orbs grew strangely dreary,
Clouded, even as they would weep.
But they wept not, but they changed not,
Never moved, and never closed;
Troubled still, and still they ranged not –
Wandered not, nor yet reposed!
So I knew that he was dying –
Stooped, and raised his languid head;
Felt no breath, and heard no sighing,
So I knew that he was dead.

('A Death-Scene', dated 2 December 1844)

A STILL, SOMBRE ATMOSPHERE descended on the parsonage in the days after Emily's death. In many ways, her final passing came as a relief to the family who had had to watch her suffer in silence, but they also knew they had lost not only a sister and daughter, but a woman the like of whom would not be seen again. Charlotte filled the days by writing letters, the only sound coming from the ticking of the grandfather clock on the staircase landing and the scratching of a nib on black-bordered mourning paper. Her letter to Ellen reporting Emily's death is particularly moving:

> Emily suffers no more either from pain or weakness now. She never will suffer more in this world – she is gone after a short, hard conflict. She died on Tuesday, the very day I wrote to you. I thought it very possible then she might be with us still for weeks and a few hours afterwards she was in Eternity – Yes – there is no Emily in Time or on Earth now – yesterday, we put her poor, wasted mortal frame quietly under the Church pavement ... the anguish of seeing her suffer is over, the spectacle of the pains of Death is gone by, the funeral day is past – we feel she is at peace, no need now to tremble for the hard frost and the keen wind – Emily does not feel them. She has died in a time of promise – we saw her torn from life in its prime.[1]

The coffin maker, William Wood, Tabby Aykroyd's nephew, later stated that the coffin he made for Emily was just 16in wide. Some have said that this would not have been out of the norm, but Wood himself said it was the narrowest he had ever made for an adult, which is even more alarming considering that Emily was much taller than the average woman of the time. It was testimony to her emaciation, and to her bravery during her suffering.

The sorrowful funeral procession was headed by Patrick Brontë, with the service itself conducted by his assistant curate, Arthur Bell Nicholls. Alongside Patrick at the head of the procession was another male who had loved Emily unreservedly: her dog, Keeper. He howled for days afterwards, and for the rest of his life he often padded disconsolately around Emily's former bedroom. Ellen Nussey recalled the sad effect the passing of his owner had on him: 'Poor old Keeper! Emily's faithful friend and worshipper – he seemed to understand her like a human ... Keeper was a solemn mourner at Emily's funeral and never recovered his cheerfulness.'[2]

There was to be no respite from illness and death at the parsonage. Within weeks of Emily's funeral, Dr Teale, of Leeds, had pronounced that Anne, the sister she had so loved, was also dying of tuberculosis. Anne took all the medicine she could for as long as she could, but eventually she could no longer keep it down. She died in her beloved Scarborough, the Yorkshire seaside resort she had visited annually when governess to the Robinsons, on 28 May 1849. By her side were Ellen Nussey and Charlotte Brontë, and as the curtain closed on her life Anne turned to her sole remaining sister and uttered her famous final words, 'Take courage, Charlotte, take courage.'[3]

Where there had been six Brontë children, now there was one, and Charlotte often found it hard to gain the courage she needed to carry on in day-to-day life. Her bilious attacks were becoming more frequent, and the recurring image of Emily's passing brought the darkest of thoughts to her mind, as we can see from the following lament:

I am free to walk on the moors – but when I go out there alone everything reminds me of the time when others were with me and then the moors seem a wilderness, featureless, solitary, saddening. My sister Emily had a particular love for them, and there is not a knoll of heather, not a branch of fern, not a young bilberry leaf not a fluttering lark or linnet but reminds me of her. The distant prospects were Anne's delight, and when I look round, she is in the blue tints, the pale mists, the waves and shadows of the horizon. In the hill-country silence their poetry comes by lines and stanzas into my mind: once I loved it – now I dare not read it – and am driven often to wish I could taste one draught of oblivion and forget much that, while mind remains, I never shall forget.[4]

The moors, poetry, the rooms within the parsonage, all brought back memories of Emily and Anne, Branwell, Elizabeth and Maria. Eventually, Charlotte found a release from her sorrows in the only way she knew how – work. *Shirley* and *Villette* were completed after Emily's death, and Charlotte also became her sisters' editor.

Smith, Elder & Co. had asked Charlotte to prepare new editions of Emily and Anne's novels and poetry to be published in 1850. It was a project she wholeheartedly embraced, as if collaborating with her sisters again. Family servant Martha Brown later recalled what a mournful sight it was to see Charlotte circling alone around the dining table at night, just as she had done years earlier with Emily and Anne by her side.

Much of Emily's poetry that can be bought today or read online is verse that has been altered by Charlotte in 1850. In some cases, she has changed a few words; in some, a few lines; in many, she has added a new title and, in some cases, most notably 'The Visionary', Charlotte has added nearly half of the poem herself, making it really a poem by Emily and Charlotte Brontë. As Emily was undoubtedly the finer poet of the two, I have trusted to her judgement, and therefore all the poems included here are taken from Emily's original manuscripts, or transcriptions thereof.

Charlotte also amended *Wuthering Heights*, mainly by changing Joseph's utterances to make them less difficult to understand for those not familiar with Yorkshire dialects.

What is most important about the 1850 editions of her sisters' work, however, is that they contained Charlotte's *Biographical Notice of Ellis and Acton Bell*, putting her sisters before the public for the very first time and finally unveiling the name of Emily Brontë. Once again, this would have been anathema for Emily, who would surely have preferred to retain her anonymity beyond the grave. She may also have found it difficult to agree with some of Charlotte's pronouncements, including her assertion:

> She [Emily] had no worldly wisdom; her powers were unadapted to the practical business of life; she failed to defend her most manifest rights, to consult her most legitimate advantage. An interpreter ought always to have stood between her and the world. Her will was not very flexible, and it generally opposed her interest. Her temper was magnanimous, but warm and sudden; her spirit altogether unbending.[5]

We should not let this be Charlotte's final verdict on Emily. It was at a time when the stoic's death, and the suffering it brought the whole family, was fresh in Charlotte's mind. Let us instead regard these lines as ones of momentary anguish, and look at the lines that directly precede them:

> In Emily's nature the extremes of vigour and simplicity seemed to meet. Under an unsophisticated culture, inartificial tastes, and an unpretending outside, lay a secret power and fire that might have informed the brain and kindled the veins of a hero.[6]

With the Bell brothers' masks firmly set aside, the Brontës quickly became a public commodity, and even in Charlotte's lifetime tourists arrived in Haworth hoping to meet her. Charlotte, although still cripplingly shy at times, embraced the life of a writer in order to dispel the black clouds of memory that lingered always on the horizon. She became feted in

London society, dining with William Thackeray, befriending Elizabeth Gaskell, and even seeing her childhood hero, the Duke of Wellington.

In June 1854, at the age of 38, Charlotte married Arthur Bell Nicholls, the man who, five and a half years earlier, had conducted Emily's funeral and then looked after her dog, Keeper. It had been a rocky courtship – an initial rejection left him threatening to become a missionary in Australia – but after the marriage Charlotte was surprised to find herself in love with her husband. One Brontë, at last, had found their happy ending, although it was a short-lived one. Charlotte quickly became pregnant but succumbed to hyperemesis gravidurum, the excessive morning sickness of which there was then little knowledge and no cure, and she died on 31 March 1855.

The Reverend Patrick Brontë had outlived his wife and all six of his children. Immensely proud of his daughters' works, he died in Haworth in June 1861, aged 84. The death scenes were at an end; the Brontë line was ended, but the lines written by Charlotte, Anne and Emily will live for ever.

Emily especially continues to captivate the imagination. As part of a writing trio, she was truly unique. Great writers will continue to appear while ever our rock continues to circle the sun, but there will never be another Emily Brontë. By reading her amazing poetry or her incredible novel, we can reach the same conclusion as Ellen Nussey, after knowing her in person, as she sat down and reflected on the life of the tall, shy woman who was only ever at home on the moors or in the parsonage next to them:

> I have at this time before me the history of a mighty and passionate soul, whom every adventure that makes for the sorrow or gladness of man would seem to have passed by with averted head. It is of Emily Brontë I speak, than whom the first 50 years of this century produced no woman of greater or more incontestable genius.[7]

Ellen has summed up the enigma at the heart of Emily Brontë's story: she created incredibly powerful writing, while at the same time living an apparently insular life untouched by the love, sorrows and gladness of others. Emily was a woman of contrasts, and a very complex person. She certainly was not morose as, although quiet, we have heard that when she wanted to she could be vivacious in conversation. She was fond of games and mischief as a child and as an adult. She was well read and a brilliant, if largely self-taught, scholar who mastered French with alarming speed, but she was also domestically adept. She was a parson's daughter who turned her back on the church, and yet she found her own spirituality centred on the natural world she saw and loved.

Emily lived an inward life, but one that was more vivid and full than the outward life of others. Driven by the huge, visionary power of her imagination, she crafted works of genius out of the whistling moorland winds. Emily Brontë was indeed a mighty and passionate soul and, like the tiny snowdrops she loved, after a brief flowering she was gone.

NOTES

Chapter 1

1 Diary of Elizabeth Firth, ms. Sheffield University Library.
2 Green, Dudley, *Patrick Brontë: Father of Genius*, p.28.
3 Wright, William, *The Brontës in Ireland*, pp.19–20.
4 Letter from Patrick Brontë to Elizabeth Gaskell, 16 June 1855, Brontë Parsonage Museum.
5 Wright, William, *The Brontës in Ireland*, pp.157–58.
6 Green, Dudley, *Patrick Brontë: Father of Genius*, p.23.
7 Barker, Juliet, *The Brontës*, p.4.
8 Interestingly, the Archbishop of York's marriage licence for Patrick and Maria lists them as much younger than they actually were, showing Patrick as 28 and Maria as 21.

Chapter 2

1 James, John, *The History of Bradford and its Parish: Volume 1*, pp.260–61.
2 Green, Dudley (ed.), *The Letters of the Reverend Patrick Brontë*, p.39.
3 *Ibid.*, p.36.
4 The uproar was reported on by the *Leeds Intelligencer*, 22 November 1819.
5 Green, Dudley (ed.), *The Letters of the Reverend Patrick Brontë*, p.43.
6 *Ibid.*, p.44.
7 Gaskell, Elizabeth, *The Life of Charlotte Brontë*, p.87.
8 Rhodes, Philip, 'A Medical Appraisal of the Brontës', *Brontë Society Transactions* (1972), p.102.
9 Orel, Harold (ed.), *The Brontës: Interviews and Recollections*, p.143.
10 Green, Dudley (ed.), *The Letters of the Reverend Patrick Brontë*, p.54.

11 A copy of these records can be found in *The Journal of Education* (January 1900), British Library, London.

12 Gaskell, Elizabeth, *The Life of Charlotte Brontë*, p.108.

13 Brontë, Charlotte, *Jane Eyre*, p.65.

14 Brontë, Emily, *Wuthering Heights*, pp.25–26.

Chapter 3

1 Gaskell, Elizabeth, *The Life of Charlotte Brontë*, p.94.

2 Barker, Juliet, *The Brontës*, p.151.

3 Orel, Harold (ed.), *The Brontës: Interviews and Recollections*, p.29.

4 Gérin, Winifred, *Anne Brontë*, p.49.

5 Leyland, Francis, *The Brontë Family*, pp.63–64.

6 Gaskell, Elizabeth, *The Life of Charlotte Brontë*, p.501.

7 *Ibid.*, p.86.

8 Brontë, Patrick, *A Sermon Preached in the Church of Haworth, on Sunday, the 12th Day of September, 1824, In Reference to an Earthquake*, ms. Brontë Parsonage Museum, Haworth.

9 Barker, Juliet, *The Brontës*, p.131.

10 *Leeds Mercury*, 11 September 1824.

Chapter 4

1 Smith, Margaret (ed.), *The Letters of Charlotte Brontë, Volume 2*, p.122.

2 Smith, Margaret (ed.), *The Letters of Charlotte Brontë, Volume 1*, p.166.

3 *Ibid.*

4 Smith, Margaret (ed.), *The Letters of Charlotte Brontë, Volume 1*, p.168.

5 *Ibid.*, p.170.

6 *Ibid.*, p.130.

7 *Ibid.*

8 Brontë, Patrick, *Cottage Poems*, p.xiii.

9 Green, Dudley, *Patrick Brontë: Father of Genius*, p.67.

10 Brontë, Patrick, *Cottage Poems*, p.34.

11 Green, Dudley, *Patrick Brontë: Father of Genius*, p.65.

12 Gaskell, Elizabeth, *The Life of Charlotte Brontë*, p.89.

13 John Greenwood's Diary, Brontë Parsonage Museum, Haworth.

Chapter 5

1 Ellen Nussey wrote a detailed account of her journey to Scarborough with Anne and Charlotte Brontë in May 1849. Entitled *A Short Account of the Last Days of Dear A.B.*, the manuscript is now in King's School Library, Canterbury.

2 Charlotte Brontë married her father's assistant curate, Arthur Bell Nicholls, in Haworth on 29 June 1854. Their engagement initially caused a rift with Ellen, but they were reconciled in time for Ellen to act as Charlotte's bridesmaid.

3 From 'Reminiscences of Charlotte Brontë' by Ellen Nussey, *Scribner's Magazine*, May 1871.

4 See Chapter 3 for an account of the explosion.

5 Diary paper of Emily and Anne Brontë, 1834, now in the Brontë Parsonage Museum, Haworth.

6 Brontë, Charlotte, *Shirley*, p.182.

7 *Ibid.*, p.279.

8 In a letter to Ellen Nussey dated 28 July 1848, Charlotte states, 'Anne continues to hear constantly – almost daily from her old pupils, the Robinsons' (original letter now at the Brontë Parsonage Museum, Haworth). This is proof that Anne, like Charlotte, must have been a voracious writer of letters.

9 See Chapter 13 for an account of Emily's time as a scholar at the Pensionnat Héger in Belgium.

10 Alexander, Christine (ed.), *Tales of Glass Town, Angria, and Gondal*, p.488.

11 *Ibid.*, p. 489.

12 *Ibid.*, p.490.

13 *Ibid.*, p.493.

Chapter 6

1 Dated 12 March 1829, Charlotte Brontë's 'History of the Year' manuscript is at the Brontë Parsonage Museum, Haworth.

2 Bovill, E.W., *Missions to the Niger*, p.75.

3 From Charlotte Brontë's 'History of the Year' manuscript, the Brontë Parsonage Museum, Haworth.

4 Barker, Juliet, *The Brontës*, p.155.

5 Branwell Brontë's *The History of the Young Men* was put onto paper in 1830–31; the manuscript is in the British Library, London.

6 This map forms the frontispiece to *The History of the Young Men*. Reproduced in Alexander, Christine (ed.), *Tales of Glass Town, Angria, and Gondal*, p.xxix.

7 Harvard University Archives, Massachusetts. A digitised copy can be seen at: https://iiif.lib.harvard.edu/manifests/view/drs:6131697$11i.

8 Emily Brontë's 'Gondal Poems' notebook, dated February 1844, ms. at the British Library, London.

9 Diary paper of Emily and Anne Brontë, 1837, now in the Brontë Parsonage Museum, Haworth.

10 Alexander, Christine (ed.), *Tales of Glass Town, Angria, and Gondal*, p.490.

11 *Ibid.*, pp.490–91.

Chapter 7

1   Leavis, F.R., *Revaluation: Tradition & Development in English Poetry*, p.6.
2   *The Guardian*, 10 August 2007.
3   Charlotte Brontë's *Biographical Notice of Ellis and Acton Bell* was published in 1850 to coincide with posthumous editions of Emily and Anne's novels. Although revealing a less than complete portrait of the sisters, it was the first time they were introduced to the public away from their Bell pen names.
4   Dated 17 October 1838, in Emily Brontë's 'Gondal Poems' notebook, ms. at the British Library, London.
5   Moore, Virginia, *The Life and Eager Death of Emily Brontë*, p.203.
6   *Ibid.*, p.205.
7   Gérin, Winifred, *Emily Brontë*, p.32.
8   *Ibid.*, p.30.
9   Butterfield, Mary A., *The Heatons of Ponden Hall*, p.19.
10 Charlotte Brontë to Ellen Nussey, 17 March 1840.
11 Smith, Margaret (ed.), *The Letters of Charlotte Brontë, Volume 1*, p.247.
12 Brontë, Charlotte, *Editor's Preface to* Wuthering Heights, British Library, London.

Chapter 8

1   See Chapter 19 for an analysis of how Anne Brontë may have brought tuberculosis back from London, leading to the deaths of Branwell, Emily and finally herself.
2   *Sheffield Independent*, 18 July 1835.
3   *Leeds Mercury*, 27 February 1925.
4   Smith, Margaret (ed.), *The Letters of Charlotte Brontë, Volume 1*, p.140.
5   *Ibid.*, p.99.
6   Alexander, Christine (ed.), *Tales of Glass Town, Angria, and Gondal*, p.162.
7   Brontë, Charlotte, *Biographical Notice of Ellis and Acton Bell*, British Library, London.
8   Smith, Margaret (ed.), *The Letters of Charlotte Brontë, Volume 1*, p.182.
9   *Leeds Times*, 23 September 1837.
10 Smith, Margaret (ed.), *The Letters of Charlotte Brontë, Volume 1*, p.182.
11 Chadwick, Ellis H., *In the Footsteps of the Brontës*, p.128.
12 *Ibid.*, p.124.
13 *Ibid.*, p.126.
14 Robinson, Agnes Mary Frances, *Emily Brontë*.

Chapter 9

1 Chadwick, Ellis H., *In the Footsteps of the Brontës*, p.124.
2 *Leeds Intelligencer*, 25 July 1846.
3 *Bradford Observer*, 10 April 1834.
4 Green, Dudley, *Patrick Brontë: Father of Genius*, pp.111–12.
5 Tyler, James, & Paul Sparks, *The Guitar and its Music: From the Renaissance to the Classical Era*, p.219.
6 The piano is now an attraction at the Brontë Parsonage Museum, Haworth. Recently restored to working order after decades as a shell, it was played by popular pianist Jamie Cullum to mark the event.
7 Brontë, Charlotte, *My Angria and the Angrians*, ms. British Library, London.
8 Barker, Juliet, *The Brontës*, p.212.
9 Orel, Harold (ed.), *The Brontës: Interviews and Recollections*, p.27.
10 Information thanks to musical scholar John Hennessy, who presented a talk entitled 'Emily Jane Brontë and Ludwig van Beethoven' in Haworth in 2014.
11 Barker, Juliet, *The Brontës*, p.150.
12 *Leeds Intelligencer*, 4 December 1828.

Chapter 10

1 Wilson, Rev. William Carus, *Want of Ministerial Success: A Sermon*, p.18.
2 Brontë, Charlotte, *Jane Eyre*, pp.25–26.
3 Gaskell, Elizabeth, *The Life of Charlotte Brontë*, p.71.
4 Greenwood, Robin, *West Lane and Hall Green Baptist Churches in Haworth in West Yorkshire*, p.93.
5 *Bradford Observer*, 9 March 1837.
6 Letter from James la Trobe to William Scruton, ms. Brontë Parsonage Museum, Haworth.
7 Brontë, Charlotte, *Jane Eyre*, p.70.
8 Lock, John, & William Thomas Dixon, *A Man of Sorrow: The Life, Letters and Times of the Rev. Patrick Brontë*, p.369.
9 Thormälen, Marianne, *The Brontës and Religion*, p.223.
10 Alexander, Christine (ed.), *Tales of Glass Town, Angria, and Gondal*, p.163.
11 Dated November 1837, ms. Brontë Parsonage Museum, Haworth.
12 Dated 10 February 1844, ms. Brontë Parsonage Museum, Haworth.
13 Dated 9 October 1845, ms. British Library, London.
14 Dated 3 February 1845, ms. Brontë Parsonage Museum, Haworth.
15 Dated 28 May 1839, ms. British Library, London.
16 Brontë, Emily, *Wuthering Heights*, pp.120–21.

Chapter 11

1 Brontë, Charlotte, *Biographical Notice of Ellis and Acton Bell*, British Library, London.

2 Letter from Charlotte Brontë to G.H. Lewes, 12 January 1848, ms. British Library, London.

3 Letter from Ellen Nussey to Elizabeth Gaskell, 15 November 1855, ms. Brotherton Library, Leeds.

4 Letter from Charlotte Brontë to W.S. Williams, 22 November 1848, ms. Brontë Parsonage Museum, Haworth.

5 Letter from Anne Brontë to Ellen Nussey, 4 October 1847, ms. Brontë Parsonage Museum, Haworth.

6 Smith, Margaret (ed.), *The Letters of Charlotte Brontë, Volume 1*, p.140.

7 Brontë, Charlotte, *The Professor*, p.74.

8 Letter from Charlotte Brontë to Emily Brontë, 2 September 1843; MacEwan, Helen, *The Brontës in Brussels*, pp.141–43.

9 Letter from Charlotte Brontë to Constantin Héger, 18 November 1845, ms. British Library, London.

10 Gaskell, Elizabeth, *The Life of Charlotte Brontë*, p.379.

11 Brontë, Charlotte, *Shirley*, p.240.

12 Brontë, Charlotte, *Biographical Notice of Ellis and Acton Bell*, British Library, London.

Chapter 12

1 Letter from Charlotte Brontë to W.S. Williams, 31 July 1848, ms. Brontë Parsonage Museum, Haworth.

2 Ellen Nussey's remembrance of Emily Brontë, ms. Brotherton Library, Leeds.

3 Brontë, Charlotte, *Shirley*, p.240.

4 Dated 12 August 1839, ms. Brontë Parsonage Museum, Haworth.

5 Gaskell, Elizabeth, *The Life of Charlotte Brontë*, p.269.

6 Brontë, Charlotte, *Shirley*, p.529.

7 Gaskell, Elizabeth, *The Life of Charlotte Brontë*, p.268.

8 Smith, Margaret (ed.), *The Letters of Charlotte Brontë, Volume 1*, p.206.

9 Gaskell, Elizabeth, *The Life of Charlotte Brontë*, p.159.

10 Barker, Juliet, *The Brontës*, p.99.

11 Diary paper of Anne Brontë, 1841, ms. Law Collection.

12 Letter from Charlotte Brontë to Rev. Henry Nussey, 9 May 1841.

13 Letter from Emily Brontë to Ellen Nussey, 16 July 1845, ms. Brontë Parsonage Museum, Haworth.

14 Letter from Emily Brontë to Ellen Nussey, 6 August 1843, ms. British Library, London.

Chapter 13

1 Diary paper of Emily Brontë, 1841, ms. Law Collection.
2 Diary paper of Anne Brontë, 1841, ms. Law Collection.
3 Letter from Charlotte Brontë to Ellen Nussey, 19 July 1841, ms. Brontë Parsonage Museum, Haworth.
4 Letter from Charlotte Brontë to Ellen Nussey, 7 August 1841, ms. Huntington Library, California.
5 Letter from Charlotte Brontë to Elizabeth Branwell, 29 September 1841; Smith, Margaret (ed.), *The Letters of Charlotte Brontë, Volume 1*, p.269.
6 Letter from Charlotte Brontë to Emily Brontë, 8 November 1841; Smith, Margaret (ed.), *The Letters of Charlotte Brontë, Volume 1*, p.273.
7 Brontë, Charlotte, *Biographical Notice of Ellis and Acton Bell*, British Library, London.
8 Brontë, Charlotte, *The Professor*, pp.43–44.
9 Gérin, Winifred, *Emily Brontë*, p.129.
10 Green, J.J., 'The Brontë–Wheelwright Friendship', *Friend's Quarterly Examiner*, Volume 50 (1916), p.123.
11 Letter from Charlotte Brontë to Ellen Nussey, July 1842 (exact date missing), ms. Huntington Library, California.
12 *Transactions and Other Publications of the Brontë Society*, Volume IV (1965), p.25.
13 Letter from Charlotte Brontë to Ellen Nussey, May 1842 (exact date missing), ms. Law Collection.
14 *Ibid.*
15 MacEwan, Helen, *The Brontës in Brussels*, p.56.
16 *Ibid.*, p.58.
17 Gaskell, Elizabeth, *The Life of Charlotte Brontë*, p.230.
18 Brontë, Charlotte, *Shirley*, p.156.

Chapter 14

1 It was a brief visit in August 1846. Emily and Charlotte consulted one of the leading eye surgeons of the day, William James Wilson. Charlotte returned with her father at the end of the month and remained in Manchester with him until he recovered from his operation.
2 Letter from Ellen Nussey to Meta Gaskell, *c.* 1855/56, ms. Brotherton Library, Leeds.
3 Barker, Juliet, *The Brontës*, p.49.
4 Unpublished ms. at Brotherton Library, Leeds.
5 *Transactions and Other Publications of the Brontë Society*, Volume VI (1965), p.142.
6 'Brontë Studies', *Journal of the Brontë Society*, Volume 27, p.20.
7 Gaskell, Elizabeth, *The Life of Charlotte Brontë*, p.96.
8 *Ibid.*, pp.96–97.

9   Brontë, Anne, *Agnes Grey*, pp.25–26.

10 Orel, Harold (ed.), *The Brontës: Interviews and Recollections*, p.25.

11 Letter from Branwell Brontë to Francis Grundy, 25 October 1842; Smith, Margaret (ed.), *The Letters of Charlotte Brontë, Volume 1*, p.294.

12 Letter from Branwell Brontë to Francis Grundy, 29 October 1842; Smith, Margaret (ed.), *The Letters of Charlotte Brontë, Volume 1*, p.295.

Chapter 15

1   Will of Elizabeth Branwell, proven 28 December 1842, National Archives, London.

2   *Ibid.*

3   See www.measuringworth.com for more details on how these figures are reached, and further calculations.

4   Gaskell, Elizabeth, *The Life of Charlotte Brontë*, pp.265–66.

5   Diary paper of Anne Brontë, 1845, ms. William Self Collection.

6   Letter from Charlotte Brontë to Ellen Nussey, 23 January 1844, ms. Law Collection.

7   Diary paper of Emily Brontë, 1845, ms. William Self Collection.

8   Letter from Charlotte Brontë to Constantin Héger, 24 July 1844, ms. British Library, London.

9   Diary paper of Anne Brontë, 1845, ms. William Self Collection.

10 Brontë, Charlotte, *Biographical Notice of Ellis and Acton Bell*, British Library, London.

11 Barker, Juliet, *The Brontës*, p.485.

12 Letter from Charlotte Brontë to Thomas de Quincey, 16 June 1847.

13 Hargreaves, G.D., 'The Publishing of Poems by Currer, Ellis and Acton Bell', *Brontë Society Transactions 1969*, p.299.

Chapter 16

1   Brontë, Charlotte, *Biographical Notice of Ellis and Acton Bell*, British Library, London.

2   Letter from Charlotte Brontë to Aylott & Jones, 6 April 1846, ms. Brontë Parsonage Museum, Haworth.

3   Diary paper of Emily Brontë, 1845, ms. William Self Collection.

4   The story of Jack Sharp and his revenge on the Walker family is contained in the Caroline Walker Diaries held at Halifax Public Library.

5   Chitham, Edward, *A Life of Emily Brontë*, p.105.

6   Brontë, Emily, *Wuthering Heights*, p.46.

7   Hogg, James, *The Private Memoirs and Confessions of a Justified Sinner*, pp.239–40.

8   *Blackwood's Edinburgh Magazine*, Volume XI (1840), pp.680–704.

9   *Ibid.*, p.704.

10 Sugden, K.A.R., *A Short History of the Brontës*, pp.26–27.

Chapter 17

1 Dated 14 September 1846, the original poem, like its reworking, is at the end of the 'Gondal Poems' notebook in the British Library, London.
2 Ms. Brontë Parsonage Museum, Haworth.
3 Gaskell, Elizabeth, *The Life of Charlotte Brontë*, p.147.
4 Letter from Ellen Nussey to Elizabeth Gaskell, 15 November 1855, ms. Brotherton Library, Leeds.
5 *The Athenaeum*, 4 July 1846.
6 *The Atlas*, 22 January 1848.
7 *Ibid.*
8 *The Examiner*, 21 January 1848.
9 The other reviews found in Emily's desk were from *The Britannia* and *Douglas Jerrold's Weekly Newspaper*, as well as a small clipping from an unknown source.
10 Letter from Charlotte Brontë to W.S. Williams, 22 November 1848.
11 Brontë, Charlotte, 'Editor's Preface to the New Edition of Wuthering Heights'.
12 Letter from Thomas Cautley Newby to Ellis Bell, 15 February 1848, ms. Brontë Parsonage Museum, Haworth.

Chapter 18

1 See the story of the masks in Chapter 3.
2 Neufeldt, Victor A. (ed.), *The Works of Patrick Branwell Brontë, Volume 3*, p.414.
3 *Ibid., Volume 1*, p.153.
4 See Charlotte Brontë's letter to Ellen Nussey, 2 July 1835.
5 Du Maurier, Daphne, *The Infernal World of Branwell Brontë*, p.47.
6 Orel, Harold (ed.), *The Brontës: Interviews and Recollections*, p.34.
7 Brontë, Emily, *Wuthering Heights*, pp.64–66.
8 De Quincey, Thomas, *Confessions of an English Opium-Eater*, p.76.
9 Barker, Juliet, *The Brontës*, p.493.
10 Orel, Harold (ed.), *The Brontës: Interviews and Recollections*, p.56.
11 Brontë, Emily, *Wuthering Heights*, p.154.
12 Du Maurier, Daphne, *The Infernal World of Branwell Brontë*, p.4.

Chapter 19

1 Letter from Branwell Brontë to J.B. Leyland, 24 January 1847, ms. Brotherton Library, Leeds.
2 Rhodes, Philip, 'A Medical Appraisal of the Brontës', *Brontë Society Transactions* (1972), p.105.
3 According to figures in the 1850 report into the health and sanitation of Haworth by government inspector Benjamin Herschel Babbage.
4 Letter from Charlotte Brontë to W.S. Williams, 31 July 848, ms. Taylor Collection, Princeton.

5   Rhodes, Philip, 'A Medical Appraisal of the Brontës', *Brontë Society Transactions* (1972), p.106.

6   Brontë, Charlotte, *Biographical Notice of Ellis and Acton Bell*, British Library, London.

7   Letter from Charlotte Brontë to Ellen Nussey, 29 October 1848, ms. Brontë Parsonage Museum, Haworth.

8   Letter from Charlotte Brontë to W.S. Williams, 2 November 1848, ms. Brontë Parsonage Museum, Haworth.

9   Letter from Charlotte Brontë to W.S. Williams, 22 November 1848, ms. British Library, London.

10 Letter from Charlotte Brontë to Ellen Nussey, 23 November 1848, ms. Brontë Parsonage Museum, Haworth.

11 Letter from Charlotte Brontë to Dr Epps, 9 December 1848, ms. British Library, London.

12 Giving the Brontë Society's annual address in July 1982, author Mary Vissick said, 'She [Emily] was always the cheerful, healthy member of a family which was cursed by persistent low-keyed ill health, so that she could not bring herself to believe that she was really ill.'

13 Barker, Juliet, *The Brontës*, p.576.

14 Gaskell, Elizabeth, *The Life of Charlotte Brontë*, p.357.

15 Letter from Charlotte Brontë to W.S. Williams, 20 December 1848, ms. Scripps College, Claremont.

Chapter 20

1   Letter from Charlotte Brontë to Ellen Nussey, 23 December 1848, ms. New York Public Library.

2   Ellen Nussey's remembrance of Emily Brontë, ms. Brotherton Library, Leeds.

3   Nussey, Ellen, *A Short Account of the Last Days of Dear A.B.*, ms. King's School Library, Canterbury.

4   Letter from Charlotte Brontë to W.S. Williams, 22 May 1850, ms. Taylor Collection, Princeton.

5   Brontë, Charlotte, *Biographical Notice of Ellis and Acton Bell*, British Library, London.

6   *Ibid.*

7   Ellen Nussey's remembrance of Emily Brontë, ms. Brotherton Library, Leeds.

SELECT BIBLIOGRAPHY

Alexander, Christine (ed.), *Tales of Glass Town, Angria, and Gondal (Introduction)* (Oxford World's Classics, 2010).

Alexander, Christine, & Jane Sellars, *The Art of the Brontës* (Cambridge University Press, 1995).

Barker, Juliet, *The Brontës* (Weidenfeld & Nicolson, 1994).

Barnard, Robert & Louise (eds), *A Brontë Encyclopedia* (Blackwell, 2007).

Bovill, E.W., *Missions to the Niger* (Cambridge University Press, 1964).

Brontë, Patrick, *Cottage Poems* (P.K. Holden, 1811).

Butterfield, Mary A., *The Heatons of Ponden Hall* (Roderick and Brenda Taylor, 1976).

Chadwick, Ellis H., *In the Footsteps of the Brontës* (Pitman, 1913).

Chitham, Edward, *A Life of Emily Brontë* (Blackwell, 1987).

De Quincey, Thomas, *Confessions of an English Opium-Eater* (Penguin, revised edition, 2003).

Du Maurier, Daphne, *The Infernal World of Branwell Brontë* (Penguin, 1972).

Gaskell, Elizabeth, *The Life of Charlotte Brontë* (Penguin Classics, 1985).

Gérin, Winifred, *Anne Brontë: A Biography* (Allen Lane, 1976).

Gérin, Winifred, *Emily Brontë* (Oxford University Press, 1971).

Gezari, Janet (ed.), *Emily Jane Brontë: The Complete Poems* (Penguin Classics, 1992).

Green, Dudley (ed.), *The Letters of Patrick Brontë* (The History Press, 2005).

Green, Dudley, *Patrick Brontë: Father of Genius* (The History Press, 2008).

Greenwood, Robin, *West Lane and Hall Green Baptist Churches in Haworth in West Yorkshire* (unpublished manuscript, 2005).

Grundy, Francis, *Pictures of the Past* (Griffith & Farrar, 1879).

Holland, Nick, *In Search of Anne Brontë* (The History Press, 2016).

Ingham, Patricia, *The Brontës* (Oxford University Press, 2008).

James, John, *Continuation and Additions to the History of Bradford, and Its Parish* (E.J. Morten, 1973).

Leavis F.R., *Revaluation: Tradition and Development in English Poetry* (Rowman & Littlefield, 1998).

Lemon, Charles, *Classics of Brontë Scholarship* (The Brontë Society, 1999).

Lemon, Charles, *Early Visitors to Haworth: From Ellen Nussey to Virginia Woolf* (The Brontë Society, 1996).

Leyland, Francis, *The Brontë Family* (Hurst & Blackett, 1886).

Lister, Philip, *Ghosts & Gravestones of Haworth* (Tempus, 2006).

Lock, John, & William Thomas Dixon, *A Man of Sorrow: The Life, Letters and Times of the Rev. Patrick Brontë* (I. Hodgkins, 1979).

Lonoff, Sue, *The Belgian Essays: A Critical Edition* (Yale University Press, 1997).

MacEwan, Helen, *The Brontës in Brussels* (Peter Owen, 2014).

Moore, Virginia, *The Life and Eager Death of Emily Brontë* (Rich & Cowan, 1936).

Neufeldt, Victor A. (ed.), *The Works of Patrick Branwell Brontë: 1837–1848* (Psychology Press, 1997).

Orel, Harold, *The Brontës: Interviews and Recollections* (Palgrave Macmillan, 1996).

Robinson, Agnes Mary Frances, *Emily Brontë* (Allen, 1883).

Smith, Margaret (ed.), *The Letters of Charlotte Brontë (Volumes 1–3)* (Clarendon Press, 1995).

Spark, Muriel, *The Essence of the Brontës* (Peter Owen, 1993).

Sugden, K.A.R., *A Short History of the Brontës* (Oxford University Press, 1929).

Tyler, James, & Paul Sparks, *The Guitar and its Music: From the Renaissance to the Classical Era* (Oxford University Press, 2007).

Wilson, Florence Romer, *All Alone: The Life and Private History of Emily Brontë* (Chatto & Windus, 1928).

Wilson, Rev. William Carus, *Want of Ministerial Success: A Sermon* (A. Foster, 1844).

Wright, William, *The Brontës in Ireland* (Hodder & Stoughton, 1894).

The versions of books by the Brontë sisters referred to in the notes are as follows:

Bell, C., E., & A., *Poems by Currer, Ellis, and Acton Bell* (Aylott & Jones, 1846).

Brontë, Anne, *Agnes Grey* (Wordsworth Classics, 1998).

Brontë, Anne, *The Tenant of Wildfell Hall* (Wordsworth Classics, 1994).

Brontë, Charlotte, *Jane Eyre* (Wordsworth Classics, 1999).

Brontë, Charlotte, *Shirley* (Collins Classics, 2012).

Brontë, Emily, *Wuthering Heights* (Penguin Classics, 1985).